# Old Testament Exegesis
## A Primer for Students and Pastors

# Old Testament Exegesis

A Primer for Students
and Pastors

Douglas Stuart

The Westminster Press
Philadelphia

*First edition*

Published by The Westminster Press®
Philadelphia, Pennsylvania

PRINTED IN THE UNITED STATES OF AMERICA

9 8 7 6 5 4 3 2 1

**Library of Congress Cataloging in Publication Data**

Stuart, Douglas K
    Old Testament exegesis.

    Bibliography: p.
    1. Bible. O.T.—Hermeneutics. 2. Bible. O.T.—
Homiletical use. 3. Bible. O.T.—Bibliography.
I. Title.
BS476.S83        221.6        80-15114
ISBN 0-664-24320-7

To
Gayle, Joanna, Eliza, and Eden

# Contents

# Abbreviations

BH³   *Biblia Hebraica,* 3d ed. (Stuttgart: Württembergische Bibelanstalt, 1937)

BHS   *Biblia Hebraica Stuttgartensia* (Stuttgart: Deutsche Bibelstiftung, 1967–1977)

LXX   The Septuagint

MT   The Masoretic Text

NT   New Testament

OT   Old Testament

# Preface

Those few students and pastors who control several ancient and modern languages, read the scholarly literature regularly, and have already gained some confidence of their ability to do exegesis will certainly not need this primer. It is written for those who cannot read a Hebrew psalm at sight and who are not sure what *Vetus Testamentum* would mean or contain (the words mean Old Testament in Latin, and are the title of a major OT scholarly journal). It is for those who have no idea what homoioteleuton might be (this term means "same kind of ending" and is a factor in certain textual problems). It is for the vast majority of all seminary students and pastors. It is predicated on the conviction that even the most intelligent people cannot understand procedures and concepts that are not somehow explained to them, and that there is no shame in seeking such explanations in spite of the fact that most seminary professors do not volunteer them. Old Testament exegesis has regular procedures and concepts, and these can be taught to almost anyone willing to learn. It is a tragedy that so few seminary students ever really feel sure of themselves in doing OT exegesis—and most pastors apparently abandon the practice altogether.

No current book in English, in my opinion, adequately addresses this need. Otto Kaiser and Werner Kümmel's *Exegetical Method: A Student's Handbook* (Seabury Press,

1963) is a good start, but it is laconic and overly general, thus ultimately not as helpful as it should be to the learner. I have set out, therefore, to present a step-by-step guide to OT exegesis that would be nontechnical and simple without being simplistic, that would explain not only the procedures but the goals of exegesis, and that would serve as a handbook for reference as the student or pastor does the actual work of exegesis.

My approach to exegesis has certain conscious biases for which I make no apologies. Perhaps the most debatable is my insistence that exegesis should include guidelines for application of the passage being studied. Exegesis is patently a theological enterprise, and a theology that is not applied to the lives of God's people is sterile. For this reason, too, I have purposely de-emphasized some of the critical techniques (e.g., structuralism, redaction criticism) which, though fascinating to the scholar, yield meager rewards theologically and are, in the final analysis, of minor value homiletically, much as that value judgment may displease some scholars. I have tried to set a fair balance between synchronic and diachronic techniques (i.e., techniques concerned respectively with the text as it stands, and the history of the developments that led to the text as it stands), but only insofar as these, too, hold promise of practical, theological benefit. The end of exegesis is preaching and teaching in the church. Seminary students and pastors know this instinctively and demand relevance from exegesis and other biblical studies, as well they should.

This primer recognizes that very few American students and pastors can read German or other scholarly languages. Of what advantage, therefore, is it to pretend that they can? The bibliographical guidance in Chapter III is thus restricted as much as possible to English works.

A unique feature of this book is found in Chapter II, which outlines an abbreviated, limited-time exegetical format for pastors. Seminary students usually learn at least in a general way how to produce formal exegesis term papers, based on dozens of hours of research and writing. But no one tells them how they can transfer that ability to the weekly preaching task, where perhaps only four or five hours may be available for the exegesis part of the sermon preparation. Exegesis can be done responsibly even if not exhaustively in a few hours' time. The pastor should first try to understand the fuller form of the guide in Chapter I. Chapter II represents a condensation and economization of that same material, with special attention paid to homiletical interests.

Those aspiring OT exegetes who know no Hebrew should still be able to make good use of the guidance given here—but there can be no denying that at least some knowledge of Hebrew is a precious advantage for student and pastor alike. I have done everything possible to encourage those whose Hebrew is weak to use it anyway. The helps discussed in Chapter III can go a long way toward overcoming the disadvantages. Indeed, the pastor who faithfully works from the biblical languages in sermon preparation, no matter how rusty his or her knowledge of them may be at the start, can't help gaining a fair language mastery as time goes by. I hope this primer will encourage many to try.

# Introduction

An exegesis is a thorough, analytical study of a biblical passage done so as to arrive at a useful interpretation of the passage. Exegesis is a theological task, but not a mystical one. There are certain basic rules and standards for how to do it, although the results can vary in appearance because the biblical passages themselves vary so much.

To do OT exegesis properly you have to be something of a generalist. You will quickly become involved with the functions and meanings of words (linguistics); the analysis of literature and speech (philology); theology; history; the transmission of the biblical writings (textual criticism); stylistics, grammar, and vocabulary analysis; and the vaguely defined yet inescapably important area of sociology. Natural intuitive skills are helpful but no substitute for the hard work of careful, firsthand research. Exegesis as a process can be quite dull. Its results, fortunately, can often be exciting. Exciting or not, the results should always at least be of genuine practical value to the believer or something is wrong with the exegesis. While this book is a primer, and hardly an exhaustive analysis of exegetical presuppositions or techniques, it ought to serve you well if your reason for learning exegesis is eventually to apply its benefits in Christian preaching or teaching.

An exegete must work from many books. Four books are

especially valuable for the methodological and bibliographical guidance they contain relating to exegesis. You should
own all four:

1. Otto Eissfeldt, *The Old Testament: An Introduction* (Harper
   & Row, Publishers, 1965).

Eissfeldt's *Introduction* contains lucid, concrete explanations of OT literary types and divisions, scholarly approaches, book-by-book content and criticism, canon and
text. There is nothing else so comprehensive or detailed,
especially in terms of its massive amount of bibliographical
guidance.

2. Frederick W. Danker, *Multipurpose Tools for Bible Study;* 3d
   ed. (Concordia Publishing House, 1970).

Danker provides backgrounds, definitions, and explanations for all sorts of books, methods, sources, and styles in
biblical exegesis. His work is the standard resource for such
information.

3. Richard N. Soulen, *Handbook of Biblical Criticism* (John
   Knox Press, 1976).

The *Handbook* is a collection of definitions. Virtually all
the exegetical terms and techniques you'll ever run across are
explained in full by Soulen.

4. Stanley B. Marrow, *Basic Tools for Biblical Exegesis* (Rome:
   Biblical Institute Press, 1976).

Marrow's *Basic Tools* is an annotated bibliography of the
lexicons, texts, grammars, concordances, and other aids used
by exegetes.
   With these four texts in hand, you'll know what the issues
in exegesis are, what kind of resources are available, and
where to find them.
   In addition to these four key books, you ought to have in
your library a copy of the Hebrew OT, a Hebrew-based
concordance, a Hebrew lexicon, a Hebrew grammar, a com-

prehensive history of Israel, a Bible dictionary, and a critical commentary series (if possible). The specific works are discussed in Chapter III. The concordance, history, dictionary, and commentary series are essential even if you don't know Hebrew. Without the proper tools, an exegesis can't go very far.

Remember as you use this guide that all the steps do not apply equally to all OT passages. For example, some passages will require major attention to historical issues and very little attention to their form or vocabulary; others will be just the opposite. There is no way to be sure of this automatically in advance. As you become familiar with a passage it will tend to become obvious to you how to assign the relative weight of each step, and the subpoints thereof.

This primer is organized into three sections. Chapter I provides a nontechnical format for term papers and other full, formal exegesis projects. Chapter II gives a simple, condensed version of the longer format, which centers especially on sermon preparation. Chapter III discusses the various exegetical aids and resources, especially bibliographical, and how to use them.

# Chapter One

# Guide
# for Full Exegesis

The outline is supplemented with large numbers of comments and questions intended to help you leave no stone unturned in doing a thorough exegesis. These comments and questions are suggestive and not to be followed slavishly. Indeed, some questions overlap and some may seem redundant to you. So be selective. Ignore what does not apply to your passage. Emphasize what does.

Pastors and others who will work mainly from the guide for sermon exegesis in Chapter II should familiarize themselves with the content of this chapter first, as it constitutes the basis for the condensation in Chapter II.

---

## OUTLINE

1. **TEXT**

   a. Confirm the limits of the passage.
   b. Compare the versions.
   c. Reconstruct and annotate.
   d. Versify poetry.

## 2. TRANSLATION

   **a.** Prepare a tentative translation.
   **b.** Check correspondence of text and translation.
   **c.** Revise.
   **d.** Provide a finished translation.

## 3. HISTORICAL CONTEXT

   **a.** Research the background.
   **b.** Research the social setting.
   **c.** Research the foreground.
   **d.** Research the geography.
   **e.** Date the passage.

## 4. LITERARY CONTEXT

   **a.** Examine literary function.
   **b.** Examine placement.
   **c.** Analyze detail.
   **d.** Analyze authorship.

## 5. FORM

   **a.** Identify the general type.
   **b.** Identify the specific type.
   **c.** Look for subcategories.
   **d.** Suggest a life setting.
   **e.** Analyze completeness.
   **f.** Be alert to partial and broken forms.

## 6. STRUCTURE

   **a.** Outline the passage.
   **b.** Look for patterns.
   **c.** Organize by size.

    **d.**  Evaluate intentionality.

    **e.**  Analyze poetic structure.

### 7.  GRAMMATICAL DATA

    **a.**  Analyze significant issues.

    **b.**  Analyze orthography and morphology.

### 8.  LEXICAL DATA

    **a.**  Explain what is not obvious.

    **b.**  Concentrate on key words.

    **c.**  Do word studies.

    **d.**  Identify special semantic features.

### 9.  BIBLICAL CONTEXT

    **a.**  Analyze use elsewhere in Scripture.

    **b.**  Analyze relation to the rest of Scripture.

    **c.**  Analyze import for understanding Scripture.

### 10.  THEOLOGY

    **a.**  Locate the passage theologically.

    **b.**  Identify issues raised or solved.

    **c.**  Analyze theological contribution.

### 11.  SECONDARY LITERATURE

    **a.**  Investigate what others have said.

    **b.**  Compare and adjust.

    **c.**  Apply discoveries.

### 12.  APPLICATION

    **a.**  Clarify the nature of the application.

    **b.**  Clarify the possible areas.

    **c.**   Identify the audience.
    **d.**   Establish the categories.
    **e.**   Determine the time focus.
    **f.**   Fix the limits.

## MOVING FROM OUTLINE TO PAPER

---

## 1. TEXT

**1.a.**  *Confirm the limits of the passage.*

Try to be sure that the passage you have chosen for exegesis is a genuine, self-contained unit (sometimes called a pericope). Avoid cutting a poem in the middle of a stanza, or a narrative in the middle of a paragraph. Your primary ally is common sense. Does your passage have a recognizable beginning and end? Does it have some sort of cohesive, meaningful content that you can observe? Check your decision against both the Hebrew text and modern translations. Do not trust the chapter and verse divisions. They are not original and are often completely wrong.

*Note:* You may find it confusing to begin with the textual analysis of your passage if your knowledge of Hebrew is not yet adequate. In that case, first prepare a rough, even wooden translation of the passage from the Hebrew. Do not delay yourself needlessly at this point. Use a trustworthy modern translation as your guide, or an interlinear if you wish (see III.2.b). Once you have a working idea of what the Hebrew words mean, you can resume the textual analysis with profit.

**1.b.   *Compare the versions.***

From as many as you can read of the Greek, Syriac, Aramaic, Latin, and Qumran versions of the passage isolate any words or phrases that do not seem to correspond to the Hebrew text you are working from. Since all of these ancient language versions have English translations (see III.2.b), you can actually work from them preliminarily even if you do not know one or more of these languages.

Refer to the critical apparatuses in BH³ and BHS, even though they are not always complete. Examine the differences (called variants). Try to decide, as best you can, whether any of the variants are possibly more appropriate to the passage (i.e., possibly more original) than the corresponding words in the Hebrew text. To do this, you must translate the variant back into Hebrew (normally via English) and then judge whether it fits the context better. Very often you can see exactly how a variant came to result from a corruption (an ancient copying mistake that became preserved in the subsequent copies) in the Hebrew text. Make these decisions as best you can, referring to critical commentaries and other aids (see III.1). All too often, especially in a poetic section, a corruption will be insoluble. The wording may not make much sense in the Hebrew as it stands, but you cannot figure out a convincing alternative. In such cases, leave the received text alone. Your task is to reconstruct *as far as possible* the text as originally inspired by God—not to rewrite it.

**1.c.   *Reconstruct and annotate the text.***

Put on paper for your reader your best guess at the original Hebrew text. Print out the reconstructed original text in full. If your reconstruction omits any words or letters from the received text, mark the omissions by square brackets: [ ]. If you insert or replace any words or letters, place the new part inside angle brackets: < >. Mark each such spot with a raised letter or number and in the footnotes explain clearly and simply your reasons for the changes. Be sure also to footnote any words you did not change but which someone else might think ought to be changed. Your reader deserves an explanation of all your significant decisions for or against changes in the text—not just those which result in actual changes.

Normally, this reconstructed text should constitute the beginning of your exegesis paper, following immediately upon the preface (if any), table of contents (if any), and introduction. Textual problems are rarely so frequent or major as to affect the sense of a passage. The rare proposed textual revision (from the MT) that materially affects the sense of the passage will probably require a major digression at this point in the paper.

**d.**   *If your passage is poetry, present it in versified form.*

In most cases you can trust BH³ and BHS to arrange the lines of poetry according to parallelism and rhythm (meter). The process of arrangement and the arrangement itself are both referred to as stichometry.

The parallelism between the words and phrases is the main criterion for deciding the stichometry. A secondary criterion is the meter (see III.6.d). If you decide upon a different stichometry for your passage from the one indicated by BH³ or BHS (their stichometries are not always right), be sure to give the reader your reasoning in a footnote. The modern English translations usually arrange poetry stichometrically. Consult them as well.

## 2. TRANSLATION

**2.a.** *Prepare a tentative translation of your reconstructed text.*

Start fresh, from the beginning. Look up in a lexicon such as Holladay's (see III.8.a) all words whose range of meaning you are not absolutely certain of. Read the more lengthy lexicon articles in major lexicons such as Koehler-Baumgartner or Brown-Driver-Briggs (see III.8.a) for significant words. Remember that words don't have a single meaning, but rather a range of meaning(s). A single Hebrew word rarely corresponds precisely to a single English word but may range in meaning through all or parts of several different English words. Translation therefore always involves selection.

**2.b.** *Check the correspondence of text and translation.*

Read your Hebrew text over and over. Know it as a friend. Memorize parts of it if possible. Read your translation over and over (out loud). Do the Hebrew and your English seem the same in your mind? Have you used a rare or complicated English word to translate a common or simple Hebrew word? If so, does the resulting precision of meaning outweigh in value the disruptive effect on the reader or hearer? Have you considered the possibility of using several English words to convey the meaning of one Hebrew word? Or vice versa? Does your passage contain words or phrases that originally were genuinely ambiguous? If so, try to reproduce rather than mask the ambiguity in your English translation. A good translation is one that creates the same general impression for the hearer as the original would, without distorting the particular content conveyed.

**2.c.**   *Revise the translation as you continue.*

As you continue to exegete your passage, especially
as you examine carefully the grammatical and lexical
data, you may learn enough to make improvements in
your tentative translation. The word(s) you choose for
a given spot in the passage should fit the overall context
well. The more you know about the whole passage, the
more feel you will have for selecting the right word in
each part. The part should fit the whole. Also, as you
make decisions about the literary and theological contexts of your passage, you will have better judgment
about the translation. Try to evaluate both the use of
a word in its broad contexts (the book, the OT, the
Bible as a whole) and its immediate contexts (your
passage, the chapter, the surrounding chapters). The
difference can be significant. For example, although
you might have assumed that the Hebrew word *bayit*
means "house" in your passage, a wider look at its uses
throughout the OT shows that in such an expression as
*bêt dāwîd* it can mean "family," "dynasty," or "lin-
eage." Which suits your passage better? Which makes
your passage clearer to the reader? By asking these
questions you help guarantee that you will not overlook
potentially useful translation options.

**2.d.**   *Provide a finished translation.*

After your research is complete and you are ready
to write the final draft, place the finished translation
immediately following the text. Use annotations (footnotes) to explain choices of wording that might be sur-
prising or simply not obvious to your reader. You are
not obliged, however, to explain any word that was also
chosen by several modern versions. Use the footnotes
to tell the reader other possible translations of a word
or phrase that you consider to have merit. Do this

especially wherever you find it difficult to choose between two or more options.

## 3. HISTORICAL CONTEXT

### 3.a. *Research the historical background.*

Try to answer the following questions in your research: What is the setting of the passage? Exactly what
events led up to this point? Did major trends or developments in Israel or the rest of the ancient world have
any bearing on the passage or any part of its content?
Are there any parallel or similar passages in the Bible
that seem to be related to the same historical conditions? Does this give any insight? Under what historical
conditions does the passage seem to have been written?
Might the passage have been written also under very
different historical conditions? If not, why not? Does
the passage bring to an end or help the progress of any
events or concepts? From this point and onward take
note of how the information you have learned about
your passage has an effect upon its interpretation. Explain how this historical information helps one to understand or appreciate the passage in some way. Be
sure to exploit any archaeological data that may exist
concerning the passage. In some instances it may not
be possible to determine the historical background of
your passage. For example, this is the case with certain
poetic passages. If so, explain this to the reader. Describe the implications of the lack of a clear historical
context, if any, for your passage.

### 3.b. *Research the social setting.*

Try to answer the following questions. Where in
Israel's life are the content or events of the passage
located? What social and civil institutions bear upon

the passage? How do they illumine the passage? Is the passage directly relevant only to an ancient Israelite (i.e., culturally "bound") or is it useful and meaningful today? Over what range of time or what breadth of Israelite (or other) culture would events of the passage (or its concepts) have been possible or likely? Are the events or concepts uniquely Israelite, or could they have occurred or been expressed elsewhere?

**3.c.**   *Research the historical foreground.*

What comes next? What does the passage lead to? What that is significant ultimately happens to the people, places, things, and concepts of the passage? Does the passage contain information that is essential to understanding something else that occurs or is said later? Is the passage at the start of any new developments? Where does the passage fit in the general scope of OT history? Are there any implications that follow from its placement?

**3.d.**   *Research the geographical setting.*

Does the passage have a provenience (a geographical setting or "origin")? In which nation, region, tribal territory, and village do the events or concepts of the passage apply? Is it a northern or southern passage? Does it have a national or regional perspective? Is it localized in any way? Do issues such as climate, topography, and economy play a role? Is there anything else about the nature of the geography that illuminates the passage's content in some way?

**3.e.** *Date the passage.*

If the passage is a historical narrative, seek the date for the events as described. If it is a prophetic oracle (revealed message), seek the date when it might have been delivered by the prophet. If it is poetry of some other sort, try to determine when it might have been composed.

Arriving at a precise date is not always possible. Be especially cautious in using secondary literature, since a scholar's critical methodology largely determines whether or not he or she will tend to consider portions of the Bible nongenuine products of a later historical period and date them accordingly.

If you cannot suggest a specific date, at least suggest the date before which the passage could not have occurred or been composed *(terminus a quo)* and the date by which the passage surely must have already taken place or been composed *(terminus ad quem).* The context and content of the passage, including its vocabulary, are your main guides to date.

Dating prophetic passages precisely is often very difficult or impossible. In most cases the only way to proceed is to try to link the message of the passage with historical circumstances known from OT historical portions and other ancient Near Eastern historical sources. Sometimes it is possible to identify a historical circumstance that forms the background for or subject of an oracle. Many times it is not, and the oracle can be dated no more precisely than within the limits of the book as a whole.

## 4. LITERARY CONTEXT

There is bound to be some overlap between the historical context and the literary context. The Old Testament is a historically oriented revelation, and therefore its progressions and orderings literarily will tend generally to correspond to the actual history of Yahweh's dealings with his people.

**4.a.** *Examine the literary function.*

Is your passage part of a story or a literary grouping that has a discernible beginning, middle, and end? Does it fill in, add on, introduce, bring to completion, or counterbalance the portion or book of which it is a part? Is it self-contained? Could it be placed elsewhere, or is it essential to its present context? What does it add to the overall picture? What does the overall picture add to it?

**4.b.** *Examine the placement.*

Just how does it fit within the section, book, division, Testament, Bible—in that order? What can you discover about its style, type, purpose, degree of literary integration, literary function, etc.? Is it one of many similar texts in the same book, or perhaps in the OT as a whole? In what sense is it unique?

**4.c.** *Analyze the detail.*

How comprehensive is the passage? If it is historical, how selective has it been? What things does it concentrate on, and what does it leave unsaid? Does it report the events from a special perspective? How does that perspective relate to the larger context? If it is poetic, how narrow or broad is its range?

**4.d.** *Analyze the authorship.*

Is the author of the passage clearly identified? Or is the passage anonymous? If anonymous, is it still possible to suggest generally the probable human source or milieu out of which God communicated his word? Is it possible that material originally written by someone else is now reused, adapted, or incorporated into a larger structure by a later inspired "writer" (usually called an editor)? Does this tell you anything theologically? Does it help you follow the logic of the passage better? If the author is known either explicitly or implicitly, does this knowledge help you connect the passage, including its motifs, style, vocabulary, etc., with other portions of Scripture from the hand of the same author? Is this in any way instructive for the interpretation of the passage? Does the author here reveal any unique features (stylistically, for example), or is the passage typical of his or her writing elsewhere?

## 5. FORM

**5.a.** *Identify the general literary type (genre).*

First locate the passage within the broad, general categories of literary types contained in the OT. Decide whether your passage is a prose type, a saying, a "song," or a combination (cf. the categories in Eissfeldt's *Introduction*—see III.1.b).

**5.b.** *Identify the specific literary type (form).*

Describe more precisely what sort of prose type, saying, or song the passage actually is. For example, if you decide that it is a historical narrative, you must then go on to judge whether it is a report, a popular

history, a general autobiography, a dream-vision account, a prophetic autobiography (here using Eissfeldt's categories), or some other specific kind of historical narrative.

You must know both the general and the specific
literary type of your passage before you are in a position
to analyze its form or forms. Only the specific—not the
general—types have "forms." That is, every specific
literary type is identifiable because it has certain recognizable features (including both outline and categories
of contents) that make it a form. For example, each
"dream account" in the OT tends to have certain features that it shares with all the other dream accounts.
The specific contents of the various dream accounts
may be different, but the features are not—each dream
account contains roughly the same *sorts* of things. They
are said to have the same form, which we call the
"dream account form."

### 5.c.  *Look for subcategories.*

The main purpose of form analysis in exegesis is that
it allows you to compare your passage with others of
like form and to exploit the knowledge that results from
that comparison. It is therefore best to describe a form
as specifically as possible without making it unique. For
example, if your passage contained a dream account
that included a conversation between an angel and a
prophet, you would probably gain more fruitful exegetical data from a comparison of your dream account
with those others which also contain a prophet-angel
dialogue, rather than with all dream accounts in general. You might even decide that tentatively you will
call your form a "prophet-angel dialogue dream account." The terminology in form analysis is not so
standardized as to rule out a certain cautiously exer-
cised freedom of terminology. However, do not try to

subcategorize your form to the extent that it becomes one of a kind. At that point it is meaningless even to speak of a form, and the benefits of comparison are lost. Those elements which cannot be compared are the special elements that call for careful attention elsewhere in your exegesis and which distinguish your passage from all others. Their uniqueness does not, however, define the form. The form is defined rather by what is typical or shared with other passages.

**5.d.** *Suggest a life setting.*

Try to link the passage (in the sense of its form or forms) with the real situation of its use. Sometimes the text itself does this for you. Otherwise, you must work inferentially and with caution. It may be obvious that a prophet has borrowed the funeral dirge form from the life situation of funerals, and reused the form in a prophetic way, e.g., singing a predictive funeral dirge for Israel, which is to be destroyed by Yahweh. But it is not so obvious where the life setting of a "community lament" psalm is to be located. Knowing the original life setting (often called the *Sitz im Leben*) usually helps you to understand the passage in a concrete way. But an overemphasis on the life setting is counterproductive. The fact that a psalm, for example, has the form of a royal accession song should not lead to the conclusion that it has no function or meaning in the OT (or among Christians today) other than as a part of the ancient Jerusalem coronation ritual. Its original setting as a form is one thing—its potential for adaptation and reuse for a whole variety of secondary settings (literary, cultural, theological, etc.) is another. Try then to balance a sensitivity to the theoretical origin of the form with its actual use in the context of your passage.

**5.e.**   *Analyze the completeness of the form.*

Compare your passage to other passages that have
the same form. In the particular instance of your passage, how completely is the given form represented?
Are all its usual elements present? If so, is there also
anything extraneous to the form that is present? If not,
what elements are lacking? Are they lacking because
the passage is logically elliptical (it leaves certain obvious elements unexpressed) or because it is purposely
modified? Does the ellipsis or modification tell you anything about what the passage is focusing on or what its
special emphases are?

Does your passage contain more than one form? If
so, how are the forms to be separated out? Does it
contain a mixture of forms or a form within a form
(e.g., a parable within a dream account)? Or, is your
passage part of a larger form, the full extent of which
goes beyond the limits of your passage? If so, what part
does your passage and its form(s) play in the greater
form?

**5.f.**   *Be alert to partial and broken forms.*

Most of the time all the known elements of a given
form will not be present in any specific instance of its
use. For example, when the prophets repeat the word
of Yahweh in the *rîb* (lawsuit) form, they often present
only one aspect such as the speech of indictment or the
judgment sentence. Presumably their audiences recog-
nized immediately from the partial form that a divine
lawsuit was being described, in the same way that we
can recognize from just the words "We interrupt this
broadcast to bring you . . ." the form used today when
an important news story is breaking. A partial form
functions to suggest the purpose, tone, style, and audience of the full form without the needless detail and

bulk necessitated by the full form. A form may also be broken (segmented) by the inclusion of other material within the form so that its constituent parts are rather widely separated from one another. Sometimes the beginning and end of a form are used to sandwich in material technically extraneous to the form proper. Such a sandwiching is known as an *inclusio.* The material sandwiched in such an *inclusio* is usually related to but not technically part of the form. Try to analyze the effect of any such structure as regards the interpretation of the passage.

*Two special cautions: historical judgments and atomization.* Considerable criticism has been leveled against two past practices of many form critics. One was the practice of calling into question the accuracy of the historical content in a given form, on the theory that certain kinds of forms preserved more genuine historical data than others. The second was the practice of assuming that the most basic forms were found in the smallest units—e.g., those of a verse or two in length—and that larger units were secondary. Both of these practices rested on assumptions that are now widely considered questionable. You should avoid them in your own exegesis.

## 6. STRUCTURE

### 6.a.  *Outline the passage.*

Try to construct an outline that genuinely represents the major units of information. In other words, the outline should be a natural, not artificial, outgrowth of the passage. Note which components are included under each topic (quantitative) and also the intensity or significance of the components (qualitative). Let the passage speak for itself. When you see a new topic, subject, issue, concept, or the like, you should construct a new topic for your outline.

After outlining the major divisions, work on the more minor divisions, such as sentences, clauses, and phrases. The outline should be as detailed as you can make it without seeming forced or artificial. From the outline you can then go on to make observations about the overall structure.

### 6.b. *Look for patterns.*

Any biblical passage whose limits have been properly identified will have a self-consistent logic made up of meaningful thought patterns. Try to identify the patterns, looking especially for key features such as developments, resumptions, unique forms of phrase, central or pivotal words, parallelisms, chiasms, *inclusio*s, and other repetitious or progressive patterns. The keys to patterns are most often *repetition* and *progression*. Look for any evidence of repetition of a concept, word, root, sound, or other identifiable feature and analyze the order of the repetition. Do the same with progressions, analyzing them as well. From this analysis may come some very helpful insights. Poetry, by its very nature, will often contain more (and more striking) structural patterns than will prose. But any passage, properly defined, has structural patterns that should be analyzed and the results interpreted to your reader. Especially point out the unexpected or unique.

### 6.c. *Organize your discussion of structure according to descending units of size.*

First discuss the overall outline pattern, usually involving not more than three to five major units. Then discuss that which you feel is important among the subpatterns within the major units, one at a time. Move from largest to smallest, i.e., from passage to paragraphs, to verses, to clauses, to words, to sounds in order. Where possible, describe whether you feel that a pattern is primary, secondary, or simply minor, and how important it is to the interpretation of the passage.

### 6.d. *Evaluate the intentionality of the minor patterns.*

Given enough time, most people can find all sorts of not very obvious minor patterns in a passage: a preponderance of certain vowel sounds here, the repetition of a verbal root there, the occurrence of a certain word exactly so many words after another word in two different verses, etc. The question is: Did these minor patterns happen to appear at random (according to the "law of averages"), or were they constructed intentionally by the ancient inspired speaker or writer? We assume that the major patterns, because they are so obvious, were intentional. We also assume that many minor patterns were intentional, especially when we can see such patterns occurring repeatedly throughout a given OT book. But how to be sure? There is only one criterion: ask whether it is likely that the ancient speaker/ writer or reader/hearer (or both) could reasonably be expected to be conscious of the pattern. If it is likely in your judgment that the answer is yes, then evaluate the pattern as an intentional one. If no, then identify the pattern as probably unintentional or the like, and be much more cautious about making exegetical inferences from it.

### 6.e. *If the passage is poetic, analyze accordingly.*

Using semantic (meaning) parallelism as the guide, arrange the lines of poetry in parallel one to another. Then attempt to identify the meter of each line. If you can, revocalize the text to reflect the original pronunci-

ation as much as possible, and describe the meter according to syllables per line (the most accurate
method). Otherwise, describe the meter according to
accents (less precise but still helpful). Note any special
metrical features or patterns. Note any groupings suggested by the metrical count. Although the concepts of
stanza and strophe are not native to Hebrew poetry,
you may divide a poem into sections or parts if such a
division actually seems to you inherent in the poem,
based upon a shift of scene, topic, or style. Rhyme or
acrostic patterns are rare but deserve careful attention
if present. Watch also for formulas (words or phrases
used in more than one place in the OT, in like metrical
contexts and patterns, to express a given idea). Formulas are the stock phrases of poetry, especially musi-
cal poetry. Compare the use of a given formula in your
passage with its use elsewhere. (See also below, step 8.)
Watch also for epiphora (repetition of final sounds or
words) and other patterns that frequently appear in
poetry. Identify any intentional instances of assonance
(repetition or juxtaposition of similar sounds), paronomasia (word play, including puns), *figura etymologica*
(variations on word roots, often involving names), and
other such poetic devices.

## 7. GRAMMATICAL DATA

**7.a.** *Analyze the significant grammatical issues.*

A correct understanding of the grammar is essential
to a proper interpretation of the passage. Are any grammatical points in doubt? Could any sentences, clauses,
or phrases be read differently if the grammar were con-
strued differently? Does your translation need revision
or annotation accordingly? Are there genuine ambiguities that make a definite interpretation of some part of
the passage impossible? If so, what at least are the

possible options? Is the grammar anomalous (not what would be expected) at any point? If so, can you offer any explanation for the anomaly? Pay attention also to ellipsis, asyndeton, prostaxis, parataxis, anacoluthon, and other special grammatical features that relate to interpretation. (See Soulen's *Handbook*—mentioned in the Introduction, above—for definitions).

**7.b.** *Analyze the orthography and morphology for date or other affinities.*

All major texts of the Hebrew Bible contain an orthography (spelling style) characteristic of the Persian period (postexilic), since the texts selected for official status by the rabbis of the first century A.D. were apparently copies from the Persian period. At many points, however, traces of older orthographies are discernible (see Cross and Freedman, *Early Hebrew Orthography* —below, III.7.b). Does the passage have any of these, or traces of special ancient morphological features? Morphology refers to meaning-affecting parts of words, such as suffixes and prefixes. (For examples, see David A. Robertson, *Linguistic Evidence in Dating Early Hebrew Poetry;* Scholars Press, 1973). If so, they may help indicate the date or even geographical origin of your passage, and may by their presence elsewhere help you to classify your passage in comparison to others. *Note:* At least an intermediate-level knowledge of Hebrew is required for this task.

## 8. LEXICAL DATA

**8.a.** *Explain what is not obvious.*

Work in descending order of size from whole clauses (if applicable) through phrases (such as idioms) to words and parts of words. Using the various helps available (see III.8), try to define for your reader any wordings or words that might not be clear, or whose force would not be noticed without attention being called to them. Some of these explanations may be very brief; others fairly detailed. Proper nouns almost always deserve some attention. When citing words from the passage, use either the Hebrew letters or an underlined transliteration of them.

### 8.b.  *Concentrate on key words and wordings.*

Working in descending order of size, isolate whatever you consider especially significant or pivotal for the interpretation of the passage. Assemble a list of perhaps six to twelve such words or wordings. Try to rank them in order from most crucial to least crucial. Focus upon these, telling your reader why they are important to the interpretation.

### 8.c.  *Do word studies of the most crucial words.*

Using the procedure outlined in III.8.c, work through the usages of a few—perhaps only one or two —of the key words in the passage. Present a summary of your procedures and findings to the reader. (Much of the statistical or procedural information may be relegated to the footnotes.) Be sure not to neglect the specific *theological* meaning(s) of words (wordings) in considering the various ranges of meaning. Be as inductive as possible, checking your conclusions against, rather than deriving them from, the theological dictionaries.

### 8.d.  *Identify any special semantic features.*

The semantics (the relation between content and meaning) of the passage is often affected by such features as anaphora, epiphora, paronomasia, metonymy,

hendiadys, formulas, loanwords, and etymological odd-
ities. Look for these, and bring them to the attention of
your reader. Where possible, show how they affect interpretation.

## 9. BIBLICAL CONTEXT

At this point you must begin tentatively drawing
together in your mind the essential discoveries from the
previous sections for the purpose of focusing on the
specific "message" of the passage, as it relates more
broadly to the message of both its immediate and its
wider context. In other words, you can no longer pay
attention only to individual features of the passage.
How the passage as a complete entity actually fits into
a broader body of truth now calls for attention.

You may find it helpful to summarize for yourself
what you consider to be the passage's message—including its central point(s), essential characteristics, unmis-
takable implications, or the like. Such a summary is
necessarily quite tentative, but it helps to focus your
attention on the biblical and theological significance of
the passage. The three procedures outlined below are
designed to help you make headway as regards the
passage's connections with the rest of Scripture, and
the three that follow in step 10 should help you relate
the passage to the more general discipline of dogmatic
theology.

### 9.a. *Analyze use of the passage elsewhere in Scripture.*

Is the passage or any part of it quoted or alluded to
anywhere else in the Bible? How? Why? If more than
once, how and why, and what are the differences, if
any? What does the reference made elsewhere to the
passage tell you about how it was interpreted? If it is

quoted, how does the circumstance under which it is quoted aid in its interpretation?

**9.b.** *Analyze the passage's relation to the rest of Scripture.*

How does the passage function dogmatically (i.e., as teaching or conveying a message) in the section, book, division, Testament, Bible—in that order? Does it have any special relationships to any apocryphal or pseudepigraphic writings? How does it or its elements compare to other Scriptures that address the same sorts of issues? What is it similar or dissimilar to?

**9.c.** *Analyze the passage's import for understanding Scripture.*

What hinges on it elsewhere? What other elements in Scripture help make it comprehensible? Why? How? Does the passage affect the meaning or value of other Scriptures in a way that crosses literary or historical lines? Does the passage concern issues that are dealt with in the same or different ways elsewhere in Scripture? What would be lost or how would the message of the Bible be less complete if the passage did not exist?

## 10. THEOLOGY

### 10.a. *Locate the passage theologically.*

Where does the passage fit within the whole corpus of revelation comprising Christian (dogmatic) theology? Under which covenant does it fit? Are aspects of it limited in part or in whole to the old covenant as, for example, certain cultic sacrificial practices would be? If so, is it still relevant as a historical example of God's relationship to human beings, or as an indication of God's standards, justice, immanence, transcendence, etc.? Is the passage related to far broader theological concerns that encompass both covenants and are not strictly bound by either? To which doctrine(s) does the passage relate? Does it have potential relevance for the classical doctrinal conceptions of God, humanity, angels, sin, salvation, the church, eschatology, etc.? Does it relate to these areas of doctrine because of its vocabulary or subject matter, or perhaps because of something less explicit? (A passage that shows the nature of the love of God for us may not happen to mention love, God, or us directly.)

**10.b.** *Identify the specific issues raised or solved by the passage.*

Go beyond the general areas of doctrine that are touched on in the passage and identify the specific issues. What in fact are the problems, blessings, concerns, confidences, etc., about which the passage has something to say? How does the passage speak to these? How clearly are they dealt with in the passage? Is the passage one that raises apparent difficulties for some doctrines while solving others? If so, try to deal with this situation in a manner that is helpful to your readers.

**10.c.** *Analyze the theological contribution of the passage.*

What does the passage contain that contributes to the solution of doctrinal questions or supports solutions offered elsewhere in Scripture? How major or minor is the passage's contribution? How certain can you be that the passage, properly understood, has the theological significance you propose to attach to it? Does your approach agree with that of other scholars or theologians who are known to have addressed themselves to the passage? How does the passage conform theologically to the entire system of truth contained in Christian theology? (It is a basic and, indeed, necessary assumption that a proper theology should be consistent overall and univocal—i.e., coherent and noncontradictory.) How does your passage comport with the greater theological whole? In what way might it be important precisely for that whole? Does it function to counterbalance or correct any questionable or extreme theological position? Is there anything about the passage that does not seem readily to relate to a particular expression of Christian theology? (Remember that the Scripture is primary, and theological systems are secondary.) What solution can you offer for any problems, even tentatively? If a solution is not readily forthcoming, why? Is it because the passage is obscure, or because you lack knowledge, or because the presumptions and speculations required would perhaps be too great to be convincing? The Bible contains some things which from a human point of view may seem difficult to comprehend, or even paradoxical. Does your passage deal with an area where there are too many unknowns to decide its theological contribution? If so, your reader deserves to be told this, but in a constructive rather than a destructive way. Do everything you can to milk the passage for its theological value, but do not force anything from or into the passage.

## 11. SECONDARY LITERATURE

**11.a.** *Investigate what others have said about the passage.*

Even though you will have consulted commentaries, grammars, and many kinds of other books and articles in the process of completing the preceding ten steps, you should now undertake a more systematic investigation of the secondary literature that may apply to your exegesis. In order for the exegesis to be *your* work and not merely a mechanical compendium of others' views, it is wise to do your own thinking and to arrive at your own conclusions as much as possible prior to this step. Otherwise, you are not so much doing an exegesis of the passage as you are evaluating others' exegeses—and therefore helping to guarantee that you will not go beyond that which they have achieved.

Now, however, is the proper time to ask what various scholars think about the passage. What points have they made that you overlooked? What have they said better? What have they given more weight to? Can you point out things that they have said that are questionable or wrong? If in your opinion other commentators are incorrect, point this out using the footnotes for minor differences and the body of the paper for more significant ones.

**11.b.** *Compare and adjust.*

Have the conclusions of other scholars helped you to change your analysis in any way? Do they attack the passage or any aspects of it in a manner that is more incisive or that leads to a more satisfying set of conclusions? Do they organize their exegesis in a better way? Do they give consideration to implications you hadn't even considered? Do they supplement your own findings? If so, do not hesitate to revise your own conclusions or procedures in steps 1 through 10, giving proper credit in each case. But never feel that you must cover in your exegesis everything that the others do. Reject what does not seem germane, and limit what seems out of proportion. You decide, not they.

**11.c.** *Apply your discoveries throughout your paper.*

Do not include a separate section of findings from secondary literature in any draft of your paper. Do not

view this step as resulting in a single block of material
within the paper. Your discoveries should produce ad-
ditions or corrections, or both, at many points throughout the exegesis. Try to be sure that a change or addition at one point does not contradict statements made
elsewhere in the paper. Consider the implications of all
changes. For example, if you adjust the textual analysis
(step 1) on the basis of your evaluation of something in
the secondary literature, how will this affect the translation, lexical data, and other parts of the exegesis? Aim
for consistency and evenness throughout. This will
affect considerably the reader's ability to appreciate
your conclusions. Give due credit to secondary sources
in the footnotes and bibliography.

## 12. APPLICATION

Everyone agrees that exegesis seeks to determine the
meaning of a passage of Scripture. Many exegetes believe that their responsibilities stop with the past: exegesis is the attempt to discover what the text *meant,*
not what it *means* now. Placing such arbitrary limits
on exegesis is unsatisfactory for three reasons. First, it
ignores the ultimate reason why the vast majority of
people engage in exegesis or are interested in the results
of exegesis: they desire to hear and obey God's word as
it is found in the passage. Exegesis, in other words, is
an empty intellectual entertainment when divorced
from application. Second, it addresses only one aspect
of meaning—the historical—as if God's words were
intended only for individual generations and not also
for us and, indeed, for those who will follow us in time.
The Scriptures are *our* Scriptures, not just the Scriptures of the ancients. Finally, it leaves the actual personal or corporate existential interpretation and use of
the passage to subjectivity. The exegete, who has come
to know the passage best, refuses to help the reader or

hearer of the passage at the very point where the reader's or hearer's interest is keenest. The exegete leaves the key function—response—completely to the subjective sensibilities of the reader or hearer, who knows the passage least. Naturally, the exegete cannot actually control what the reader does in response to the passage. But the exegete can—and must—do his or her best to define the areas within which a faithful response will be found, and to suggest, if necessary, areas of response which the passage might seem on the surface to call for but which are not justified by the results of the exegesis.

The key to proper application of a passage is *comparing life issues.* To apply a passage you must try to decide what is the central issue and what are the secondary issues with which the passage is concerned. What aspect(s) of life is the passage concerned with? Then you must try to decide whether such issues are still active in the lives of persons or groups today. What do "I" or "we" encounter today that is similar or at least related to what the passage deals with? From there one can proceed to decide whether or not the passage provides any insight or guidance that would be helpful to the person or group for whom such issues are a matter of concern. Making these decisions about application is definitely more a matter of qualitative art than of quantitative science. Nevertheless, the following procedural steps will help you isolate the life issues of the passage systematically; they will maximize your chances of relating these life issues properly to the life issues of persons or groups for whom an exegesis of the passage should have benefit.

In the application process you have three inter-related basic concerns. First, you need to know the life issues raised in the passage. These should emerge from the exegetical data. Second, you need to identify which issues or concepts are transferable from the passage to the current situation. This necessitates properly integrating and harmonizing the exegetical data from the passage with theology, both biblical and dogmatic. Third, you need to apply these issues or concepts accurately, by understanding current life issues. This depends on your knowledge of the audience for whom you do the exegesis, as well as on your own God-given self-understanding. The questions that follow here move to some extent between these three concerns, in a way that is intended to help you sort them out as objectively as possible.

**12.a.** *Clarify the nature of the application.*

Applications may generally be of two kinds: those which basically *inform* the reader and those which basically *direct* the reader. A passage that functions to describe some aspect of the love of God might be considered primarily to inform. A passage that functions to command the reader to love God wholeheartedly primarily directs. Obviously there is considerable overlap between informing and directing, and a passage can contain elements that are at the same time informative and directive. Nevertheless the force of your application will be much clearer and more specific if you divide the applicability in this way, at least tentatively. At first, maximize—include all the possibilities, knowing that you will discard some or most later, after more analysis. Caution: Narrative passages do not generally teach something directly; rather, they illustrate what is taught directly elsewhere.

**12.b.** *Clarify the possible areas of application.*

Applications may fall into two general areas: *faith* and *action.* In practice, faith and action should ultimately be inseparable—a genuine Christian could not display one without the other. But even though they must belong together in the Christian's life, faith and action are nevertheless distinct entities, and a given passage, part or whole, may concentrate on one more than the other. Try therefore to decide the potential areas of application for the material contained in the passage, dividing tentatively into categories of faith and action. Be inclusive at first; reject and discard later.

**12.c.** *Identify the audience of the application.*

There are primarily two audiences to whom the application(s) may be seen to be directed: the personal and the corporate. What in the passage gives information or direction regarding faith or action to individuals? What to groups or corporate structures? If such a differentiation cannot be made, why not?

If the passage informs or directs individuals, what kind of individuals are they? Christian or non-Christian? Lay persons or clergy persons? Parents or children? Powerful or weak? Haughty or humble? What in the passage makes this clear? How does the passage address the object of its informing or directing? If the passage informs or directs groups or corporate entities, which kind are they? Church? Nation? Clergy? A profession? A societal structure? Some other group or combination of groups?

**12.d.** *Establish the categories of the application.*

Is the application directed toward matters that are primarily interpersonal in nature? Matters that relate to piety? To the relationship of God and people? Is the concern social, economic, religious, spiritual, familial, financial, etc.?

**12.e.** *Determine the time focus of the application.*

Does the passage call primarily for a recognition of something that occurred in the past? Does it expect present faith or action? Does it look primarily to the future? Does the application involve a combination of times?

**12.f.** *Fix the limits of the application.*

Does the passage call for a response that could possibly be misunderstood and taken too far? If so, how can you define what is too far? Does the passage call for an application that is secondary rather than primary? That is, does your passage function more as a background or support, or part of a further or larger passage which more specifically suggests an application than does your passage? Is your passage one of several that all function together to suggest a given application which none of them individually would quite have? Are there any applications which at first might seem appropriate to the passage but which upon more careful examination are not? If so, briefly identify these for your reader and give your reasoning. It is often at least as crucial to explain how a passage does not apply than to explain how it does. Does the passage have a double application, as for example certain messianic passages do—one application having immediate reference, the other having more of a long-range reference? If so, are both applications of equal weight now? Were they of equal weight when the passage was first spoken or written?

In general, it is probably safest to limit potential applications as much as possible. Rare is the passage that calls for several applications, all of equal relevance or practicability. Try to decide what *one* application is most central to and follows most naturally from the passage. If you are absolutely convinced that the passage demands more than one application, at least try to rank these in order of either universality of application or urgency of application. Remember: You are not responsible to discuss all the possible ways in which the passage might strike the fancy of the reader or be put to use by the reader. Rather, you are responsible to inform the reader what the passage *itself* calls for or leads to in terms of application. If the passage is so brief or specialized that you are at a loss to suggest any application for it (even as part of a greater whole), you would be wiser to suggest no application than to suggest one that is ultimately unsound.

## MOVING FROM OUTLINE TO PAPER

After completing the research in step-by-step fashion, you will naturally be concerned to organize the results into a format that presents them effectively to the reader.

There are many acceptable formats. If a given one is specified for you by a professor or editor, you will obviously follow that. Otherwise you might wish to consider using one of the three most common options. The first is the topical format, which proceeds much in the same order as the twelve steps above, but with sections and headings rearranged, combined, expanded, or otherwise adjusted according to your own best sense of how the material of the passage can convincingly be drawn to the attention of the reader. The second is the commentary format, which moves more or less verse by verse through the passage, marshaling relevant data and conclusions as they apply to individual parts of the passage, yet not excluding appropriate additional sections such as introductions, excursuses, summaries, etc. The third is the unitary format, in which the passage is discussed in a relatively free-flow-ing fashion, apart from a strictly systematic or methodical outline, with or without the use of formally identified sections, subsections, headings, etc.

Any of these formats—and many others—can serve you well. Do not hesitate to be innovative, as long as the format you choose aids in getting the full impact of your findings across to your readers.

# Chapter Two

# Short Guide
# for Sermon Exegesis

This short guide is intended to provide the pastor with a handy format to follow in doing exegetical work on a passage of Scripture for the purpose of preaching competently on it. Each section of the guide contains a suggestion of the approximate time one might wish to devote to the issues raised in that section. The total time allotted is somewhat arbitrarily set at about five hours, the minimum that a pastor ought normally to be able to give to the research aspect of the sermon preparation. Depending on the particular passage, the time available to you in any given week, and the nature of your familiarity with exegetical resources, you will find that you can make considerable adjustments in the time allotments. If you are new to exegetical preaching, you will need to increase the time allotments substantially.

As you become increasingly familiar with the steps and methods, you may arrive at a point where you can dispense with reference to the guide itself. This is the intention of this primer—that it should get you started, not that it should always be needed.

*OUTLINE*

## 1. TEXT AND TRANSLATION

   **a.** Read repeatedly.
   **b.** Check for textual issues.
   **c.** Make your own translation.
   **d.** Compile a list of alternatives.
   **e.** Start a sermon use list.

## 2. LITERARY-HISTORICAL CONTEXT

   **a.** Examine background.
   **b.** Describe literary-historical setting.
   **c.** Examine foreground.

## 3. FORM AND STRUCTURE

   **a.** Identify genre and form.
   **b.** Investigate life setting of forms, where appropriate.
   **c.** Look for structural patterns.
   **d.** Isolate unique features and evaluate.

## 4. GRAMMATICAL AND LEXICAL DATA

   **a.** Note important grammar.
   **b.** List key terms.
   **c.** Pare down the list to manageable size.
   **d.** Do a mini word study.

## 5. BIBLICAL AND THEOLOGICAL CONTEXT

   **a.** Analyze use elsewhere in Scripture.
   **b.** Analyze relation to Scripture.
   **c.** Analyze relation to theology.

## 6. APPLICATION

   **a.** List life issues.
   **b.** Clarify nature and area of application.
   **c.** Identify audience and categories.
   **d.** Establish time focus and limits.

## MOVING FROM EXEGESIS TO SERMON

---

### COMMENT

Most pastors who are theologically trained have been required to write at least one exegesis paper during their seminary days. Many have written Old Testament exegesis papers, based on the Hebrew text. But few have been shown how to make the transition from the exegetical labor and skills required for a full term paper to those required for a sermon. The term paper necessitates substantial research and writing, is in many ways narrow and technical, and involves the writer in the production of a formal, typed manuscript to be evaluated by a single professor, with special attention to methodological competence and comprehensiveness, including notes and bibliography. The sermon is usually composed in ten hours or less (total), must avoid being excessively narrow or technical, does not require a formal manuscript, is evaluated by a large and diverse group of listeners who are mostly not scholars and who are less interested in methodological competence than in the practical results thereof.

Because the format and the audience are so radically different, is it any wonder that pastors find it hard to see the connection between what they were taught in seminary and what they are expected to do in their study and in the pulpit? Is it any wonder, too, that the average Sunday sermon is so often either devoid of exegetical insight or sprinkled with exegetical absurdities that countless congregations across the land long in vain for "simple preaching from the Bible"? The pastor, having long ago abandoned any hope that his or her weekly schedule would allow for the same sort of high-quality exegesis involved in writing the term paper, has nothing to put in its place. As a result, no exegesis is done. The sermon becomes a long string of personal illuminations, anecdotes, truisms, platitudes, and whatever general insights the commentaries may provide.

The latter are usually far removed from the specific comprehension level and practical concerns of the congregation hearing the sermon. The pastor stands in the ideal position between scholarly research and practical living, but cannot bring the one to bear upon the other. After all, how can the time be found week by week to devote oneself to the extensive research on which a truly exegetical sermon would be based? Both pastor and congregation suffer for want of a method to bridge the gap, a method almost never taught in the seminaries.

The Short Guide for Sermon Preparation is a blended version of the full guide used for exegesis papers. Although the process of exegesis itself cannot be redefined, the fashion in which it is done can be adjusted considerably. Exegesis for sermon preparation cannot and, fortunately, need not be as exhaustive as that for the term paper. The fact that it cannot be exhaustive does not mean that it cannot be adequate. The goal of the shorter guide is to help the pastor extract from the passage the essentials pertaining to sound hermeneutics (interpretation) and exposition (explanation and application). The final product, the sermon, can and must be based on research that is reverent and sound in scholarship. The sermon, as an act of obedience and worship, ought not to wrap shoddy scholarship in a cloak of fervency. Let your sermon be exciting, but let it be in every way faithful to God's revelation.

**1. TEXT AND TRANSLATION** *(Allow approximately one hour.)*

**1.a.** *Read the passage repeatedly.*

Go over the passage out loud, in the Hebrew if possible. Try to get a feel for the passage as a unit conveying God's word to you and your congregation. Go over the passage out loud in English as well. (Use a modern translation, unless you and your congregation insist upon using the King James Version. In the latter case you must be doubly careful to pay close attention to step d, below.) Try to become sufficiently familiar with the passage so that you can keep its essentials in your head as you carry on through the next five steps. Be on the lookout for the possibility that you may need to adjust somewhat the limits of your passage, since the chapter and verse divisions as we have them are secondary to the composition of the original and are not always reliable. Check by starting a few verses before the beginning of the passage, and going a few verses past the end. Adjust the limits if necessary (shrink or expand the passage to coincide with more natural boundaries if your sense of the passage so requires). Once satisfied that the passage is properly delimited, and that you have a preliminary feel for its content and the way its words and thoughts flow, proceed to step 1.b, below.

**1.b.** *Check for significant textual issues.*

Refer to the textual annotations in either the Kittel *Biblia Hebraica* (BH[3]) or the *Biblia Hebraica Stuttgartensia* (BHS) at the bottom of the Hebrew page. Look specifically for text variations that would actually affect the meaning of the text for your congregation in the English translation. These are the major textual vari-

ants. There is not much point in concerning yourself
with the minor variants—those that would not make
much difference in the English translation. By referring
to one or two of the major technical commentaries
which address issues of text and translation (see III.2.f)
you can quickly check to see if you have correctly
identified the major variants. Finally, you must evaluate the major variants to see whether any should be
adopted, thus altering the "received" text (the Masoretic text as printed in the Hebrew Bible). If you cannot
make a decision—often the commentators cannot either—then you may wish to draw this to the attention
of your congregation. In this regard see also steps 1.d
and 1.e, below.

**1.c.** *Make your own translation.*

Try this, even if your Hebrew is dormant or weak.
You can easily check yourself by referring whenever
necessary to one or two of the respected modern versions. Avoid referring to the nonliteral paraphrases
(even though some are called "versions" or "translations"), since these will tend to confuse you without
helping much. They are confusing because they do not
usually represent a direct rendering of the Hebrew original and are thus hard to follow. They will not help
much because they are useful primarily for skimming
large blocks of material to get the gist—rather than for
close, careful study where, to some degree, each word
(and just the right word) is important. You may also
refer for translating help to an interlinear version (see
III.2.b).

Making your own translation has several benefits.
For one thing, it will help you to notice things about
the passage that you would not notice in reading, even
in the original. It is a little like the difference between
how much you notice while walking down a street as

opposed to driving down it. Much of what you begin to notice as you prepare your translation will relate to steps 2–6, below. For example, you will probably become especially alert to the structure of the passage, its vocabulary, its grammatical features, and some aspects of its theology, since all these are drawn naturally to your attention in the course of translating the words of the passage. Moreover, you are the expert on your congregation. You know its members' vocabulary and educational level(s), the extent of their biblical and theological awareness, etc. Indeed, you are the very person who is uniquely capable of producing a meaningful translation that you can draw upon in whole or in part during your sermon, to ensure that the congregation is really understanding the true force of the word of God as the passage presents it.

**1.d.** *Compile a list of alternatives.*

If the passage does contain textual or translational difficulties, your congregation deserves to be informed about them. The congregation can benefit from knowing not just which option you have chosen in a given place in the passage, but what the various options are and why you have chosen one over the other(s). They can then follow some of your reasoning rather than accepting your conclusions "on faith." The best way to prepare this for the sermon is by way of a list of alternatives for both the textual and the translational possibilities. Only significant alternatives should be included in each list. You may expect your list to contain at most one or two textual issues, and a few translational issues. In the sermon itself, you can easily work these alternatives into the discussion of what the text says by such introductions as: "Another way to read this verse would be . . ." or "We could also accept a possible original wording of the text which reads . . ." A short summary of why you feel the evidence leads to your choice (or why you feel the evidence is not decisive) can be provided or not, depending on the demands of time.

**1.e.** *Start a sermon use list.*

In the same manner as you compiled the list of alternatives mentioned in 1.d, above (and perhaps including that list), keep nearby a sheet of paper on which you record those observations from your exegetical work on the passage which you feel are worth mentioning in your sermon. This list should include points discovered from all of steps 1–6, and will provide an easy reference as you construct the sermon itself.

What to include? Include the very things that *you* would feel cheated about if you did not know them. They need not be limited to genuine life-changing observations, but they should not be insignificant or arcane either. If something actually helps you appreciate and understand the text in a way that would not otherwise be obvious, then put it down on the mention list.

Maximize at first. Include anything that you feel deserves to be mentioned because your congregation might profit from knowing it. Later, when you actually write or outline your sermon, you may have to exclude some or most of the items on the mention list, by reason of the press of time. This will be especially so if you choose to make your sermon dramatic, artistic, stylized, or the like, thus departing more or less from a rigidly expository format. Moreover, in perspective you'll undoubtedly see that certain items originally included for mention are not so crucial as you first thought. Or, conversely, you may find that you have so much of significance to draw to your congregation's attention that you will need to schedule two sermons on the passage to exposit it properly.

Remember: Your mention list is not a sermon outline, any more than a stack of lumber is a house. The mention list is simply a tentative record of those exegetically derived observations that your congregation deserves to hear and may indeed benefit from knowing.

## 2. LITERARY-HISTORICAL CONTEXT *(Allow approximately one hour.)*

### 2.a. *Examine the background of the passage.*

There is usually considerable overlap between the literary context and the historical context of an Old Testament passage. Nevertheless, it is helpful to attempt to identify whether some feature is *primarily* literary or *primarily* historical. Accordingly, you should first attempt to identify the general literary background of the passage. Refer to OT introductions (see III.11.e) and commentaries (III.11.f) as necessary. If it is narrative, what preceded it in the narrative? If it is one of a group of stories, which stories came before, and how do they lead up to the passage? If it is a prophetic oracle, which oracles serve to introduce or orient the passage in any way? Try to isolate both the *immediate* background (preceding paragraphs or sections of the book in which the passage occurs) and the *general* background (the relevant literary materials from any prior time in OT history).

Proceed in the same manner with the historical background, referring to the OT histories (see III.3.b) as needed. Look first for the immediate background and then for the overall background. Be sure your congregation has a sense of what happened before—of what related events and forces God superintended that set the stage for the passage. Some passages, of course, do not have much of a discernible historical background. Psalm 23, for example, cannot easily be tied to any specific events in the psalmist's (or Israel's) past.

This psalm, however, does have features that are important with regard to its setting (see 2.b, below).

You cannot hope to be exhaustive in your analysis of the literary-historical background of the passage in the modest time available to you for your sermon preparation. Therefore, you must be selective in two ways. First, concentrate on the highlights. Select those literary features and historical events which seem to you most clearly and obviously important for the congregation to be aware of. Eliminate from consideration aspects of the passage's literary and historical background which if omitted would not materially affect the ability of your congregation to understand or interpret the passage. In other words, you are searching for the essentials—those things which need to be pointed out in order to represent the background of the passage fairly. These must be *representative* rather than comprehensive. Secondly, summarize. In some cases, you may not be able to spare more than a minute or two of your sermon to discuss the background of a passage. Try then to construct a brief summary of the background information that sets the scene for the passage in its immediate and then its overall contexts according to the broad sweep of things.

### 2.b. *Describe the literary-historical setting.*

To have described the background (2.a, above) and the foreground (2.c, below) of your passage is a major aspect of describing the context, but there is more. You should also be sure your congregation has some sense of the literary *setting* in terms of placement and function as well as authorship, and the historical *setting* in terms of social, geographical, and archaeological coordinates, as well as actual chronological coordinates (date).

*Placement and function.* Where does it fit in the

section, book, division, Testament, Bible? Is it introductory? Does it wind up something? Is it part of a group of similar passages? Is it pivotal in any way? What sort of a gap would its absence leave?

*Authorship.* Who wrote it? Is it clearly attributed to someone, or is it anonymous? Is there dispute about the authorship? Does (or would) knowing the authorship make any difference? If the author is known, what else did he or she write? Is the passage typical or atypical of the author's work? Are there known characteristics of the author that help make the passage more comprehensible?

*Social setting (including economic and political setting).* What in the life of Israel at this time would help your congregation to appreciate the passage? Does the passage touch on or reflect any social, economic, or political issues, customs, or events that should be mentioned? Under what personal, family, tribal, national, and international conditions and circumstances were the events or ideas of the passage produced?

*Geographical setting.* Where was it written? Where did the events take place? Do these make any difference in understanding the passage? Would the passage be different if it were written or its events took place elsewhere? How important is the geographical setting— marginally or centrally? If no setting is given, is this fact significant or merely incidental?

*Archaeological setting.* Consult the Scripture quotation index of one or more of the OT archaeologies (III.d), histories, and commentaries. Is there anything specifically available from archaeological research that relates to the passage itself or to its relatively immediate context? If there is, does it provide a helpful perspective in any way?

*Date.* Wherever possible, give the absolute and relative dates for any event(s) or person(s) in the passage, or for the literary production ("original publication") of the passage. Most churchgoers know few dates. They aren't sure whether Ruth comes before or after David, or whether Esther comes before or after Abraham, or in what century to locate any of them. The more often you take the time to explain the dates related to a passage (it need not take very long, after all), the more clear the interrelationships of people, books, and events will become to your congregation. God's revelation to us is a historical one—do not neglect chronology.

**2.c.** *Examine the foreground of the passage.*

What follows immediately, both literally and historically? What comes next in the chapter(s) following? Is it something that relates closely to the passage or not? How does it relate and what help, if any, does it give for understanding the passage? What follows immediately? Are there any events known to have taken place soon afterward that may shed light on the passage? Using the OT histories, check to see if there are aspects of Israelite or ancient Near Eastern history that are not covered (or not covered in detail) in the Bible that nevertheless may help show the import of the passage. Is there anything that occurs relatively soon afterward that might be significant for your congregation to know? Even though an event might not be a result of, or affected by, something mentioned in the passage, are there any events that are similar or logically (even if not causally) related? Follow the same process with the longer-range literary and historical foreground. Try to describe what follows in the book, division, Testament, and Bible that may be of genuine relevance to the passage. Do the same for the historical aspect. Don't hesitate to bring matters right up to or beyond current times, if legitimate. (For example, an OT prophecy about the kingdom of God might well include ancient Israel, the current church, and the heavenly, future kingdom.)

In general, you want to avoid talking to your congregation about the passage in isolation, as if there were no Scripture or history surrounding it. To do so is to be unfair to the sweep of the historical revelation; it suggests to your congregation that the Bible is a collection of atomistic fragments not well connected one to another and without much relationship to the passage of time. That is surely not *your* conception of the Bible, and it should likewise not be the impression that you leave with your parishioners. Try to pay attention to those things (even in summary) which will help them realize that God has provided us with a Bible which can be appreciated for the whole as well as the parts; and that God controls history *now,* thus controlling *our* history with the same loyalty that he showed to his people in OT times.

## 3. FORM AND STRUCTURE *(Allow approximately one half hour.)*

### 3.a. *Identify the genre and the form.*

Your congregation deserves to know whether the passage is in prose or poetry (or both), whether it is a narrative, a speech, a lament, a hymn, an oracle of woe, an apocalyptic vision, a wisdom saying, etc. These various types (genres) of literature have different identifying features, and, more importantly, must be analyzed with respect to their individual characteristics lest the meaning be lost or obscured. For example, consider the preaching of Jonah, "Yet forty days, and Nineveh shall be overthrown!" (Jonah 3:4). Your congregation will likely be puzzled as to why Jonah, the Nineveh hater, should have wanted to avoid preaching such an obviously negative message of doom, unless you explain to them that the possibility of repentance and therefore forgiveness is *implicit* in this warning of delayed pun-

ishment. The knowledge of the form and its characteristics leads to the knowledge that Jonah is actually,
though reluctantly, preaching a message of hope to
Nineveh. It is not essential that you identify every form
by its technical name, but you should try to be sure that
you identify the overall type of literature (e.g., prophetic) and then the form used in the passage (e.g., the
warning oracle), since in most cases such an identification will serve to enhance the appreciation and the
interpretation of the passage.

**3.b.** *Investigate the life setting of forms, where appropriate.*

If there are any discernible links between the form(s)
used in the passage and real-life situations, identify
these for your congregation. The "watchman's song"
used to describe the destruction of Babylon from the
vantage point of a sentry (Isa. 21:1–10) has its greatest
impact when the congregation is reminded that in ancient times the watchman or sentry on the city wall was
often the first person to see something coming and thus
to announce news of significant events. Since the
prophet, too, is Yahweh's announcer of news or events,
the imagery of Isaiah's oracle in ch. 21 is especially
appropriate. A knowledge of the original life setting
from which the form is borrowed for reuse is often
crucial to grasping its significance. Explain these factors to your congregation, and the prophetic message
can come across to them with much the same force
with which it came across to Isaiah's original audience.
You do not need to give a detailed form-critical analysis
of the text to your congregation; but you should at least
go by the principle that they ought to hear anything
about the form(s) that would enhance their grasp of the
message. To do less is to leave the congregation partly
in the dark. Where possible, let your congregation in on
anything that helps *you* follow the meaning.

### 3.c. *Look for structural patterns.*

Outline the passage, seeking to discover its natural flow or progression. How does it start; how does it proceed; how does it come to an end? How does the structure relate to the meaning? Is the message of the passage (or at least the impact of the message) at least partly related to the structure? What is the "logic" of the passage, and what interpretational clues can you discern in its logic?

Then look specifically for patterns. Are there any repetitions of words, resumptions of ideas, sounds, parallelisms, central or pivotal words, associations of words, or other patterns that can help you get a handle on the structure? Look especially for evidence of repetitions and progressions which may help you to understand what the passage is emphasizing. How exactly has the inspired writer ordered his or her words and phrases, and why? What is stressed thereby? What is brought full circle to completion? Is there anything especially beautiful or striking in the structure, especially if the passage is a poem? Remember that the structure not only contains the content but is also to some extent *part of* the content. Structures can be quite prominent (as in Genesis 1) or quite unobtrusive (as in some stories of Israelite Kings), but they are usually significant.

### 3.d. *Isolate unique features and evaluate their significance.*

Form criticism and genre criticism emphasize the typical and universal features that are common to all instances of a given type or form of literature. Structural criticism and rhetorical criticism, on the other hand, are concerned more with the unique and the specific in a particular passage. Both are needed. You need to appreciate a passage for what it shares in com-

mon with similar passages, but also for what it alone
contains that specially characterizes it, that makes it
different. In terms of the general structure, and also in
terms of the repetitions and progressive patterns, what
do you find in the passage that gives it a distinct flavor
—that describes the passage itself on its own terms and
according to its own topics and concepts? What particular revelatory content is communicated within and
beyond just the general form(s) and genre(s) which the
passage contains or is part of?

## 4. GRAMMATICAL AND LEXICAL DATA   *(Allow ap-
proximately 50 minutes.)*

**4.a.**  *Note any grammar that is unusual, ambiguous, or otherwise important.*

Your primary interest is to isolate grammatical features that might have some effect upon the interpretation of the passage. Anything that can be explained—
at least in some general way—is fair game for the congregation. But do not address yourself to minutiae.
Find the major, significant anomalies, ambiguities, and
cruxes (features crucial for interpretation) if any. Few
passages contain many of these, so the task should not
take long.

Ambiguities deserve special explanation. If a
prophet reports that Yahweh has a word '*al y<sup>e</sup>rû-
šālaim,* for example, your congregation will profit from
knowing this can mean "about Jerusalem," "on behalf
of Jerusalem," or "against Jerusalem." The translations must choose one of these options—they cannot
include all three, and thus cannot accurately represent
the ambiguity in the passage, which in many cases is a
suspenseful ambiguity. The audience of the ancient
prophet could not always tell whether Yahweh's word
was good or bad until the prophet ended the suspense

by further words. Cruxes certainly deserve special attention: If the interpretation of the passage (or a doctrine mentioned by the passage) depends upon taking some grammatical feature a certain way (e.g., "You shall have no other gods *before me*"), this should be explained clearly so that no question is left about the proper interpretation. ·

**4.b.** *Make a list of the key terms.*

As you go through the passage, write down all the English words (sometimes phrases) that you consider important. These may include verbs, adjectives, nouns, proper nouns, etc. Include anything that you are not sure that a majority of your congregation could define, as well as any terms they might want to know about. A typical passage of ten or fifteen verses might yield a dozen words or more. For example, the story of Abijah's speech and battle against Jeroboam in II Chron. 13:2b–18 yields the following key words and phrases that the average congregation might either know relatively little about or might benefit from having exposited to them: Abijah, Jeroboam, thousand, Mount Zemaraim, hill country of Ephraim, all Israel, covenant of salt, servant of Solomon, Rehoboam, the sons of David, golden calves, sons of Aaron, Levites, consecrate, no gods, burnt offerings, incense of sweet spices, showbread, golden table, golden lampstand, forsaken, battle shout, relied, God of their fathers.

**4.c.** *Pare down the list to manageable size.*

Because of the demands of time, you must be selective. Decide whether you can include five, ten, or perhaps more of the key terms in your inclusion list. Retain the terms that you are sure your congregation needs to learn about (perhaps: "covenant of salt," "consecrate," "no gods," "relied," "God of their fathers," etc., from the sample above). Eliminate what is not central to the needs of your sermon, as well as you can predict this (perhaps "thousand," the place names, the offering names, the names of temple furnishings, "battle shout," etc., from the sample above). You may find that some important points of your sermon will suggest themselves in the process of deciding what to comment on and what to leave with minimal or no comment. From the sample passage above, for example, you might pick "A Covenant of Salt" as your sermon title. That ought to arouse at least a little advance curiosity about the sermon.

**4.d.**  *Do a mini word study of at least one word or term.*

Any sensibly chosen passage will contain at least one word or term worthy of investigation beyond the confines of the passage. Force yourself to the weekly discipline of picking a word or term and sampling its usage and therefore its range(s) of meaning first in the section, then the book, then the division, then the Testament, then the whole Bible. Use the techniques for word study described in III.8.c, but use your time wisely: Check the various contexts in English if you wish; know what to look for by seeking guidance from the lexicons and published word studies. But whatever you do, get beyond the immediate context of the passage. Let your congregation hear something about that word or term as it is used *throughout* the Bible as best you can summarize the evidence in the short time you have.

## 5. BIBLICAL AND THEOLOGICAL CONTEXT *(Allow approximately 50 minutes.)*

**5.a.** *Analyze use of the passage elsewhere in Scripture.*

Evaluate those cases where any part of the passage is quoted elsewhere in the Bible. How and why is it quoted? How is it interpreted by the quoter? What does that tell you about the proper interpretation of the passage?

**5.b.** *Analyze the passage's relation to the rest of Scripture.*

How does it function? What gaps does it fill in? What is it similar or dissimilar to? Is it one of many of similar types, or is it fairly unique? Does anything hinge on it elsewhere? Do other Scriptures help make it comprehensible? How? Where does it fit in the overall structure of biblical revelation? What value does it have for the student of the Bible? In what ways is it important for your congregation?

**5.c.** *Analyze the passage's use in and relation to theology.*

To what theological doctrines does the passage add light? What are its theological concerns? Might the passage raise any questions or difficulties about some theological issue or stance that needs an explanation? How major or minor are the theological issues upon which the passage touches? Where does the passage seem to fit within the full system of truth contained in Christian theology? How is the passage to be harmonized with the greater theological whole? Are its theological concerns more or less explicit (or implicit)? How can you use the passage to help make your congregation more theologically consistent or, at least, more theologically alert?

**6. APPLICATION**   *(Allow approximately one hour.)*

**6.a.**   *List the life issues in the passage.*

Make a list of the possible life issues that are mentioned explicitly, referred to implicitly, or logically to
be inferred from the passage. There may be only one or
two of these, or there may be several. Be inclusive at
first. Later you can eliminate those which, upon reflec-
tion, you judge to be less significant or irrelevant.

**6.b.**   *Clarify the possible nature and area of application.*

Arrange your tentative list (mental or written) according to whether the passage or parts of it are in
nature informative or directive, and then whether they
deal with the area of faith or the area of action. While
these distinctions are both artificial and arbitrary to
some degree, they are often helpful. They may lead to
more precise and specific applications of the Scripture's
teaching for your congregation, and they will help you
avoid the vague, general applications that are sometimes no applications at all.

**6.c.**   *Identify the audience and categories of application.*

Are the life issues of the passage instructive primarily to individuals or primarily to corporate entities, or
is there no differentiation? If to individuals, which?
Christian or non-Christian? Clergy or lay? Parent or
child? Strong or weak? Haughty or humble? If to corporate entities, which? Church? Nation? Clergy? Laity?
A profession? A societal structure?

Are the life issues related to or confined to certain
categories such as interpersonal relationships, piety,
finances, spirituality, social behavior, family life?

**6.d.** *Establish the time focus and limits of the application.*

Decide whether the passage primarily calls for a recognition of something from the past, a present faith or action, or hope for the future; otherwise, perhaps a combination of times is envisioned. Then set the limits. Your congregation would be well served by suggestions of what would be extreme applications, lest they be inclined to take the passage and apply it in ways or areas that are not part of the intentionality of the Scripture. Is there an application that is primary while others are more or less secondary? Does the passage have a double application as, for example, certain messianic passages do? If so, explain these to your congregation and suggest where *their* responsibilities to the informing and directing of the passage lie.

In suggesting applications, it is generally advisable to be cautious. Avoid especially the principle of imitation (the idea that because someone in the Bible does it, we can or ought to do it, too). This is the most dangerous and irreverent of all approaches to application since virtually every sort of behavior, stupid and wise, malicious and saintly, is chronicled in the Bible. Yet this monkey-see-monkey-do sort of approach to applying the Scriptures is very widely followed, largely because of the dearth of good pulpit teaching to the contrary. To be cautious involves staying with that which is certain, and shying away from the questionable (possible but uncertain) applications. You are not responsible to suggest to your congregation all the possible ways in which a passage might be applied. You *are* responsible to your congregation to explain the application which is clearly and intentionally the concern of the passage. Unless you are convinced that it is the *intention* of the Scripture that it be applied in a certain way, no suggestion as to application can be confidently advanced. It would be far better to admit

to your congregation that you have no idea how the
passage could be applied to their lives than to invite
them to pursue an application devoid of legitimate
scriptural authority. In all likelihood, however—if
your passage is sensibly chosen and your exegetical
work properly done—you will be in a position to suggest in your sermon confidently and in a practical way
not only what the passage means but what it should
lead you and your congregation to believe and do.

## MOVING FROM EXEGESIS TO SERMON

There are many ways to prepare sermons and to
deliver them, many different types of sermons and
books about them. Still, some general advice can be
given about creating a sermon that is exegetically
sound.

**a.**    *Work from your sermon use list.*

Organize the various notes on your list into categories. See how many fit together. Do some groups seem
especially weighty? For example, does much of the list
seem to center on theological terms and themes? If so,
perhaps your sermon ought to be especially theological.
Does the list contain many elements that are part of a
story? If so, might not the sermon take a story form?
Will you need to explain a good many lexical items? If
so, perhaps a number of illustrations will be required,
and so on. Generally, the material on the sermon use list
should at least suggest what some of the major blocks for
building the sermon will be, whether or not it suggests a
particular format for the sermon. Remember, too, that
you probably will not be able to include (or at least to
cover adequately) in the sermon everything you placed
tentatively on the sermon use list. Discard what you
must. A single sermon cannot do everything.

**b.** *Do not use the exegesis outline as the sermon outline.*

You will surely not last long in the pastorate if your congregation hears every sermon begin with: "Let us examine the textual problems of the passage . . ." The six-point exegetical outline provides an orderly and incremental format for covering the exegetical issues of a passage. It is not a sermon outline. You must organize and incorporate the results of your exegesis into the sermon according to an order which has as its primary concern to educate and challenge the congregation. It is up to you to decide what sort of a sermon, containing what elements in what order, will best convey this to the listeners—and no one is in a better position to make such a decision than you are.

**c.** *Differentiate between the speculative and the certain.*

Let your congregation know which exegetical "discoveries" are possible, which are probable, and which are definite. You may be excited by the possibility that a particular poetic couplet in Hosea seems to be adapted from Amos, but you would be irresponsible to present this as a given, since equally plausible cases can be built that Amos did the borrowing, or that both prophets drew upon a common repertoire of prophetic poetry, or that they were independently inspired with a similar message, etc. There is no harm in alerting your congregation to any or all of these options as long as you identify them as speculative.

**d.** *Differentiate between the central and the peripheral.*

The sermon should not give equally high priority to all exegetical issues. The fact that you may have spent a half hour trying to get straight a particularly tricky historical problem of Israelite-Assyrian chronology does not mean that ten percent of the sermon should therefore be given over to an explanation of it. You may well choose not to mention it at all. Try to decide what the congregation *needs* to know from the sermon passage, as opposed to what you needed to know to prepare the sermon. There is much they can do without. Your two best criteria for making this decision are the passage itself and your own reactions to it. What the passage treats as significant is probably what the sermon should treat as significant; what you feel is most helpful and important to you personally is probably what the congregation will find most helpful and important to them.

**e.**  *Trust the homiletical commentaries only so far.*

Most pastors rely far too heavily on the so-called homiletical commentaries (those which emphasize suggestions for preaching) and not enough on their own scholarly exegesis. This can be counterproductive, since the homiletical commentaries are for the most part exegetically shallow. In addition, since the commentator has no personal knowledge of you and your congregation, he or she cannot possibly provide other than general observations and insights. The commentator can hardly speak to the controversies, the special strengths and weaknesses, the hot topics, the ethnic, familial, social, economic, political, educational, interpersonal, and other concerns that constitute the particular spiritual challenges for you and your congregation. The commentator has no idea how much or how little your congregation knows about a given topic or passage, how much ground you intend to cover in your sermon, or even the size of the units of the passage you have chosen to preach on. Accordingly, you are advised to refer to homiletical commentaries for the supple-

mental insights they may offer you after, not before,
you have done the basic work yourself.

**f.** *Remember that application is the ultimate concern of a*
*sermon.*

A sermon is a presentation designed to apply the
word of God to the lives of people. Without application, a talk is not a sermon; it may be a lecture, a lesson,
or the like, but it is not a sermon. Be sure that you
construct a sermon that does not neglect a clear, practi-
cable, and exegetically based application. This does not
mean that most of the time given to the sermon must
be spent on the application. The major proportion of
time, in fact, may be spent on matters that are not
strictly applicational, as long as they help lay the
ground for the application. Indeed, you can hardly
expect your congregation to accept your suggested application of a passage solely on your own authority.
They need to be shown how the application is based on
a proper comprehension of the passage's meaning, and
they will probably not take the application to heart
unless this is clear to them. Likewise, you must not
merely explain to them what it *says* while avoiding
what it *demands*. The Bible is not an end in itself—it
is a means to the end of loving God with one's whole
heart and loving one's neighbor as oneself. That is what
the law and the prophets are all about.

Reference to the secondary literature is always necessary. There are too many specialized issues and
sources for interpreting those issues for the student (or
the professional scholar, for that matter) to rely only
upon his or her methodology. To properly interpret a
portion of the book of Job, for example, one must have
some understanding of the special ways in which
Canaanite myths are used, reused (albeit "sanitized"),
and otherwise employed in the service of the message

of Yahweh's sovereignty over all creation. Likewise, the special (Northern Canaanite) dialect used in Job is simply beyond the ken of the seminary student whose only Semitic language is Hebrew. One must of necessity turn to the specialists for help, and often even for an awareness of what the exegetical issues are. No one's work may be accepted uncritically, however. Specialists display poor judgment and a willingness to accept unlikely conclusions as often as anyone else. They are capable of giving plausibility to their poor judgments and unlikely conclusions by surrounding them with large amounts of related data and erudite verbiage. Nevertheless, your own common sense and your right to remain unconvinced, until such time as you are shown facts and arguments that seem to you convincing, will serve you well. Your main concern when facing difficult, specialized issues that require expertise beyond your own is not to *originate,* but to *evaluate.* Look critically at what the specialists are saying, compare their logic and their data, and choose from among them what seems most convincing. No one can ever ask more of you.

# Chapter Three

# Exegesis Aids
# and Resources

The helps and bibliographical referrals in this chapter are arranged according to the outline for the full guide in Chapter I. With a few necessary exceptions, the books recommended are limited to those available in English. The best books, in terms of relevancy as well as technical expertise, are listed, regardless of theological slant. However, in the case of OT and Christian theologies (section 10), some attention is paid to differing theological viewpoints.

---

*OUTLINE*

1. **TEXTUAL CRITICISM**

    a. The Need
    b. Explanations
    c. The Versions
    d. Critical Text Editions
    e. Word-by-Word Version Comparison
    f. The Footnotes in BH³ and BHS
    g. The Masora
    h. Other Masoretic Indicators

2. **TRANSLATION**

   **a.** Translation Theory
   **b.** Translation Aids

3. **HISTORY**

   **a.** General Chronology
   **b.** Israelite History
   **c.** Other Parts of the Ancient Near East
   **d.** Archaeology
   **e.** Geographies and Atlases
   **f.** Historical Criticism
   **g.** Tradition Criticism

4. **LITERARY ANALYSIS**

   **a.** Parallel Literature
   **b.** Genre Criticism
   **c.** Redaction Criticism
   **d.** Literary Criticism
   **e.** Source Criticism
   **f.** Dating

5. **FORM**

   **a.** Form Criticism
   **b.** The Relationship of Form to Structure

6. **STRUCTURE**

   **a.** Definitions
   **b.** Rhetorical Criticism
   **c.** Formula Criticism
   **d.** Poetry Analysis

## 7. GRAMMAR

- **a.** Reference Grammars
- **b.** Other Technical Sources

## 8. LEXICAL ANALYSIS

- **a.** Lexicons
- **b.** Concordances
- **c.** Word Studies
- **d.** Theological Dictionaries
- **e.** Inscriptions

## 9. BIBLICAL CONTEXT

- **a.** Chain Reference Lists
- **b.** Topical Concordances
- **c.** Commentaries and Biblical Context
- **d.** Apocrypha and Pseudepigrapha
- **e.** The Old Testament in the New

## 10. THEOLOGY

- **a.** Old Testament Theologies
- **b.** Christian Theologies

## 11. SECONDARY LITERATURE

- **a.** Special Reference Sources
- **b.** The Journals
- **c.** Old Testament Introductions
- **d.** Commentaries
- **e.** Bible Dictionaries
- **f.** Other Aids

**12. APPLICATION**

    **a.** Hermeneutics
    **b.** Some Do's and Don'ts

---

## 1. TEXTUAL CRITICISM

**1.a.** *The Need for Textual Criticism*

    Many pastors and students find textual criticism boring and cannot imagine that it could be more than marginally significant to biblical studies. Boring it may sometimes be—so are many important and necessary scholarly tasks. However, the proper selection of textual readings may be quite significant to the interpretation of a passage, and cannot therefore be avoided. Even those OT books which are relatively free from textual problems—the Pentateuch, Judges, Esther, Jonah, Amos, etc.—still present the reader with textual choices in virtually every chapter. And those books well known for their frequent textual corruptions— Hosea, Ezekiel, Samuel-Kings, Psalms, Job, Zechariah, etc.—can often require of the exegete textual decisions affecting the interpretation of a majority of the verses in a given passage! The task of textual criticism may seem unappealing, even annoying; but it is unavoidable.

    There is no single authoritative version of the Old Testament text in existence. The Hebrew text printed in BH³ and BHS (see III.f) is merely a copy of the Leningrad Codex, a manuscript from the eleventh century A.D., one manuscript among many from ancient and medieval times. Because the formats of BH³ and BHS provide for the printing of this manuscript in full with a selection of alternative readings (wordings) given in the footnotes, the impression is given that the readings in the footnotes are somehow irregularities, i.e., minor deviations from the norm or standard given in the full, printed text. This is simply not so. The alternative readings (called variants) are themselves only a selection of the possible different readings from a great variety of ancient manuscripts of the Old Testament in various languages, each of which was considered both authoritative and "standard" by some community of faith at some time in the past. The choice to print one particular eleventh-century manuscript by reason of its good state of preservation and relatively early date is not wrong—but it can be misleading. If a slightly earlier medieval manuscript had been in the same good state of preservation, it would have been chosen for printing, even though its readings might be different at many hundreds of places throughout the OT. In other words, the variants given in the footnotes of BH[3] and BHS, along with the many other variants not mentioned by the rather selective editors of those editions, should be accorded fair consideration along with the Leningrad Codex. Many times, perhaps even a majority of times, they are more likely to preserve the original Hebrew wordings than the Leningrad Codex is. The variants represent the many other ancient copies of the OT which may also reflect the original text. In any given instance (at any given point in the OT text) any one of them could be right and all the others that differ could be wrong. Each case must therefore be decided on its own merits even if, as is well known, certain copies and versions are considered *generally* less reliable than others.

There are many differences between the various versions and many obvious corruptions (ungrammatical, illogical, or unintelligible wordings) within given manuscript traditions or "recensions." Moreover, outnumbering the obvious corruptions are the "hidden" corruptions—those which subsequent copyists reworked into wordings that seem on their surface faultless but are shown to be unoriginal when the full information from a variety of versions is analyzed.

Because textual criticism can be fairly complicated, and because decisions about original wordings are often subjective, you may be tempted to say: "I won't make any decisions at all about the text. I'll work exclusively from my Masoretic Text." In so doing, however, you will have made thousands of decisions automatically. You will have everywhere in the OT chosen the Masoretic readings of the Leningrad Codex, some of which are best, but some of which are the very worst. You will commit yourself to interpreting garbled and incoherent sentences and verses—easily clarifiable by reference to the other versions. And you will, at least tacitly, insult the intelligence of the original human author, as well as the Holy Spirit's inspiration of the text, by accepting uncritically the sometimes nonsensical, sometimes too short, sometimes too long MT when fruitful, helpful alternative readings are available if you are willing to expend the necessary labor to look them up and evaluate them. By the way, doing textual criticism not only sharpens your knowledge of Hebrew, Greek, and any other relevant languages you may read, it also helps involve you in the basic exegetical decisions about the text. A "likely" reading is decided partly by appeal to the general nature, structure, vocabulary, and theological message of the text. So doing your textual criticism thoroughly will involve doing your exegesis well. To decide against doing any textual criticism is to decide already that certain exegetical issues are beyond you—to give up the fight, as it were, before you start.

**1.b.** *Explanations*

The best introduction to OT textual criticism is a short (84 pp.), easy-to-read book which explains the

procedures, the versions, and the evidence in a not
overly technical way:

> Ralph W. Klein, *Textual Criticism of the Old Testa-
> ment;* Guides to Biblical Scholarship (Fortress
> Press, 1974).

A much longer introduction to the subject is found
in:

> Ernst Würthwein, *The Text of the Old Testament*
> (Oxford: Basil Blackwell, Publisher, 1957; rev.
> ed., Wm. B. Eerdmans Publishing Co., 1979).

This book emphasizes texts and versions. In some
ways, it is largely a companion volume to BH³, explain-
ing what the various texts are, where they originate,
and something of their history. The greater part of the
book is devoted to reproduction (with very helpful explanations) of forty-one important manuscripts. It is
not as useful as Klein's work, however, for actually
learning how to do textual criticism.

Also very helpful for its clear, detailed definitions
and explanations on texts and versions and their relevance to OT textual criticism (but not so much on the
method of textual criticism itself) is:

> Frederick W. Danker, *Multipurpose Tools for Bible
> Study;* 3d ed. (Concordia Publishing House,
> 1970).

A convenient and remarkably thorough source of
information on texts and versions, with attention to the
individual books, is found in Part Five of Eissfeldt's
*The Old Testament: An Introduction.* Its special value
lies in the copious references to books and articles on
the various topics:

> Otto Eissfeldt, *The Old Testament: An Introduction*
> (Harper & Row, Publishers, 1965).

Also convenient, though considerably more general,
is:

> R. K. Harrison, *Introduction to the Old Testament*
> (Wm. B. Eerdmans Publishing Co., 1969).

This work contains in Part Four ("The Old Testament
Text and Canon") not only a survey of the history of
Hebrew writing but some judicious evaluations of the
limits and fruits of textual criticism. Harrison provides
along with each book's introduction a brief description
of its textual characteristics and notable problems.

For easy access to clear and practical definitions of
terms, alphabetically listed, see:

Richard N. Soulen, *Handbook of Biblical Criticism*
(John Knox Press, 1976).

A famous example of careful textual criticism applied to a large section of the OT is:

S. R. Driver, *Notes on the Hebrew Text and the
Topography of the Books of Samuel;* 2d ed. (Oxford: Clarendon Press, 1913).

### 1.c.  *The Versions*

In addition to the Masoretic Text (MT), one copy of
which is printed as the basis of BH³ and BHS, there are
five other main ancient versions of the OT in four languages. Listed in descending order of importance they
are:

*The Greek OT.* Called the Septuagint (LXX), this
version represents a translation from the Hebrew in the
third century B.C. Its importance cannot be minimized.
On the average, it is just as reliable and accurate a
witness to the original wording of the OT (the "auto-
graphs") as the MT is. In many sections of the OT, it
is more reliable than the MT; in others, less. Largely
because the Greek language uses vowels and Hebrew
does not, the LXX wordings were less ambiguous and
the LXX was inherently less likely to be marred by
textual corruptions than the Hebrew, which went on
accumulating corruptions (as well as editorial expansions, etc.) for many centuries after the LXX was produced. When you undertake textual criticism (except in

certain sections of the OT which books like Klein's
identify), you should probably place the LXX side by
side with the MT, and treat them as equals.

*The Qumran copies.* These are the Dead Sea Scrolls
of the OT. In some cases, e.g., Isaiah and Habakkuk,
large portions are preserved in a Hebrew text that is
pre-Christian and thus many centuries earlier (and
more reliable) than anything previously known. However, for most books only small fragments have been
found. Chances are, therefore, that your passage will
not have a corresponding Qumran text. If it does, however, you may generally treat the Qumran wording as
equal in reliability to the MT wording.

*The Syriac OT.* Called the Peshitta, the Syriac OT
is sometimes (but far less often than the LXX) a useful
witness to the Hebrew text from which it was translated
(and revised) several centuries after Christ. Frequently
when it differs from the Hebrew MT, it does so in
agreement with the LXX.

*The Aramaic OT.* Called the Targum, the Aramaic
OT is occasionally important as an indication of the
original Hebrew, but is often marred by expansionism
and a tendency to paraphrase excessively. Like the Syriac Peshitta, it is a relatively late witness.

*The Latin OT.* Jerome's translation of the Hebrew
OT into Latin (389 to 405 A.D.), called the Vulgate, is
the only ancient Latin translation that has survived in
full. Only rarely is it an independent witness to anything other than the MT, since it was produced from
a version that we would call essentially an early or
proto-MT.

Naturally you will be limited to the use of those
versions which are in a language you know. Otherwise
you must depend on those critical commentaries which
pay attention to textual criticism (such as *The Anchor
Bible,* the *Hermeneia* series, and the old but very useful
*International Critical Commentary*—see III.11.d).

Fortunately, nearly all the crucial data for making intelligent textual decisions are located in the Hebrew and Greek, the languages most likely to have been studied during one's seminary training.

### 1.d. *Critical Text Editions*

*The LXX.* After being produced, the LXX was copied and recopied many hundreds of times, just as the Hebrew OT was. All this copying over many centuries provided ample opportunity for different readings to develop, both as a result of accidental miscopyings (corruptions) and as expansions and other "editorial" work on the part of scribes. As a result, critical Greek texts have been required. These contain a single fully printed text, copious footnotes indicating the "inner-Greek" variants (those variants which result from Greek texts in transmission without any regard for the Hebrew), footnotes indicating the revision-produced variants (those variants which were introduced by conscious harmonizing of a given LXX copy to some Hebrew copy available to and trusted by the reviser); and footnotes giving information from other language versions.

Two major multivolume critical editions of the LXX now exist. Each series is incomplete, but the two together largely complement each other so that almost the entire OT is covered:

> Alan E. Brooke, Norman McLean, Henry St. J. Thackeray, *The Old Testament in Greek* (Cambridge University Press, 1906–1940).

The following books are available in this series: Genesis through II Chronicles (following the English order), I Esdras, Ezra-Nehemiah, Esther, Judith, Tobit. The other series is:

> *Septuaginta: Vetus Testamentum Graecum Auctoritate Societatis Litterarum Gottingensis Editum*

(Göttingen: Vandenhoeck & Ruprecht, 1931– ).
The following books are included in this series:
Esther, I, II, III Maccabees, Psalms *(Psalmi cum Odis)*, Wisdom of Solomon *(Sapientia Salomonis)*, Sirach *(Sapientia Iesu Filii Sirach)*, The minor prophets *(Duodecim Prophetae)*, Isaiah *(Isaias)*, Jeremiah *(Jeremias)*, Baruch, Lamentations *(Threni)*, The Letter of Jeremiah *(Epistula Jeremiae)*, Ezekiel, Susanna, Daniel, Bel and the Dragon *(Bel et Draco)*.

Both of the above series use Latin as the means of communication, as do BH³ and BHS.

Unlike the NT texts, none of the OT critical editions in either Hebrew or Greek produces an eclectic text (a text that is made from the best possible choices from among all the variants). The production of an eclectic text is thus up to you. Using the aids at your disposal, you are at least not likely to do worse than the existing MT (called sometimes the "received text"), and may well improve upon it.

Also helpful is a comprehensive listing of books and articles written on the Septuagint (thus mostly on text-critical issues), which allows for quick recourse to the relevant studies of the various books and passages:
Sebastian P. Brock, Charles T. Fritsch, Sidney Jellicoe, *A Classified Bibliography of the Septuagint* (Leiden: E. J. Brill, 1973).

*The Dead Sea Scrolls.* The various texts are published in a variety of sources. Most are so fragmentary as to be useless exegetically. For a complete list of the publications, see Fitzmyer, *The Dead Sea Scrolls* (III.11.f). A superb photographic reproduction of the two most nearly complete OT texts from Qumran (Isaiah and Habakkuk, the latter being included in an ancient commentary) is found in:
*Scrolls from Qumran Cave I from Photographs* by John C. Trever (Jerusalem: The Albright Institute

of Archaeological Research and The Shrine of the Book, 1974).

*The Peshitta.* A critical edition of the text is under way, but thus far comprises only small portions of the OT:

*The Old Testament in Syriac,* ed. by the Peshitta Institute of Leiden (Leiden: E. J. Brill, 1972– ).

The most widely available full copy is an uncritical edition, usually obtainable from Bible societies:

*Vetus Testamentum Syriace et Neosyriace* (Urmia, 1852; repr. London: Trinitarian Bible Society, 1954).

For other editions, see Eissfeldt's *The Old Testament: An Introduction,* section 120 (above, III.1.b).

*The Targum.* The standard edition is now:

Alexander Sperber (ed.), *The Bible in Aramaic;* 4 vols. (Leiden: E. J. Brill, 1959–1973).

*The Vulgate and Vetus Latina.* For both the Vulgate and its predecessor the *Vetus Latina* (Old Latin) there are critical editions, based in the latter case on those few portions which still survive. Eissfeldt's *The Old Testament: An Introduction* (see III.1.b) gives a complete list of the editions, in sections 123 and 124. There are inexpensive editions of the Vulgate available. The most common is:

Alberto Colunga, Laurentio Turrado (eds.), *Biblia Vulgata* (Madrid: Biblioteca de Autores Cristianos, 1953; repr. 1965).

### 1.e. *Word-by-Word Version Comparison*

To analyze the various versions of the OT, you must in effect translate each one back into Hebrew at least to the extent that you can tell it reflects the MT or runs contrary to the MT. Since this can be complicated, it may be helpful to chart the versions one above another, line-by-line, so that your ability to compare readings is facilitated. Remember to compare the wording of the versions for the whole passage. If you try to consult the versions only when the MT seems problematic, you will miss all the variants that resulted from MT corruptions that once were obvious but later were smoothed over and rewritten into readable Hebrew (but not necessarily the original Hebrew) by well-meaning scribes.

A word-by-word comparison in the case of I Sam. 20:32 (where the Qumran version happens to exist) would look something like the chart on the next page.

By writing out the Hebrew of the MT, then listing selected versions (including the LXX) directly underneath, according to the Semitic word order from right to left, you can easily see how the versions line up. In the example above, the parentheses are a convenient way to indicate that both the Qumran text and the LXX omit any correspondence to the MT אליו , suggesting that this word might be an expansion (in this case, a simple explanatory addition) in the MT. However, the LXX also omits any correspondence to the MT and Qumran words: אביו ויאמר . This perhaps reflects a haplography (a loss of something once present) in the Hebrew text that was used by the LXX translator. The Peshitta and Targum follow the MT, as they usually do. The Vulgate, typically, follows the MT.

In the example above we have included the English translation according to the Semitic word order. You may find it helpful to do this, at least at first. You may also wish to include the English translation under any spot where the versions contain a different wording from the MT, especially if you cannot translate the various versions at sight! Refer to Klein's *Textual Criticism of the Old Testament* (see III.1.b). In Chapter 5 ("Doing Textual Criticism"), he gives many other helpful examples and explanations of the principles in-

# I Samuel 20:32

| Hebrew | English | MT | Qumran | LXX | (MT) Syriac | (MT) Targum | (MT) Vulgate |
|---|---|---|---|---|---|---|---|
| ויען | And answered | | [first two words obliterated] | Kai apekrithē | " | " | " |
| יהונתן | Jonathan | | [first two words obliterated] | Iōnathan | " | " | " |
| את שאול | Saul | | " | tō Saoul | " | " | " |
| אביו | his father | | " | ( ) | " | " | " |
| ויאמר | and said | | " | ( ) | " | " | " |
| אליו | to him | | " | ( ) | " | " | " |
| למה | Why | | " | Hina ti | " | " | " |
| יומת | must he die? | | " | apothnēskei | " | " | " |
| מה | What | | " | ti | " | " | " |
| עשה | has he done? | | " | pepoiēken | " | " | " |

volved in deciding which version best reflects the original.

### 1.f. The Footnotes in BH³ and BHS

In BH³ (the "Kittel" edition) there are two separate paragraphs of footnotes. The upper paragraph contains information on variants that are thought by the editors to be of relatively minor importance. They are indicated in the text by small Greek letters. The lower paragraph, indicated by small Latin letters, contains what the editors thought was most significant, including suggestions for actual correction of the MT toward a more likely original. Sometimes the editor does nothing more than record the evidence from the various versions and manuscripts, leaving any decision about changing the text up to the reader. At other times, the editor will actually suggest how the MT should be corrected or at least report what a commentator has suggested by way of a change (emendation). The explanations are given in Latin abbreviations. A convenient English key to those abbreviations and to the signs and major versions is found in a valuable little pamphlet widely available:

> Prescott Williams, Jr., "An English Key to the Symbols and Latin Words and Abbreviations of *Biblia Hebraica*" (Stuttgart: Württembergische Bibelanstalt, 1969).

In the new BHS (the "Stuttgart" edition) there are also two separate paragraphs. The upper paragraph, set in very small type, contains notations related to the Masoretic apparatus printed in the margins (see III.1.g). The lower paragraph combines and updates the kinds of notations that were grouped into two separate paragraphs by the BH³ editors. In general, the BHS textual notes are superior to those of BH³ but are still neither exhaustive nor always definitive.

The critical apparatus in both BH³ and BHS will
help you to see at a glance some of the evidence for
certain obvious textual issues, but they are no substitute
for your own comprehensive word-by-word check of
the versions in a full exegetical analysis of a passage.

### 1.g. *The Masora*

Printed in the margins of both BH³ and BHS are
groups of notations written in Aramaic and mostly
abbreviated, made by the Masoretes. Some notations
may suggest possible improvements upon the text, but
most indicate observations useful to the accurate pres-
ervation and copying of the text. In the ancient Masoretic manuscripts many of these notes were placed in
the margins. These were called the *masora parva*, "the
little Masora." Longer notations were placed at the
beginning or the end of the manuscripts. These were
called the *masora magna*, "the large Masora." For
most purposes of exegesis, the Masora itself is paid little
attention by scholars because its truly significant observations are already incorporated into the notes in BH³
and BHS, or can be duplicated by quick reference to a
concordance. Moreover, such observations have been
rendered unnecessary by the development of the print-
ing press. In other words, it is quite common to ignore
the Masora in doing exegesis. You will be in good
company to do so.

### 1.h. *Other Masoretic Indicators*

The Masoretes produced a dots-and-dashes vowel
pointing system so that their students, for whom Hebrew was by then a dead language, could pronounce the
words properly (i.e., properly according to the postbib-
lical pronunciation that had evolved by the sixth to
ninth centuries A.D.). In addition, they developed ac-

cent marks, other marks to indicate verse divisions and sections thereof, and notations for such things as Scripture portions used in the yearly cycle of synagogue readings. None of these markings or notations, including the vowel pointing system, represents anything more than the opinion of the Masoretes according to their own early medieval, and often conflicting, traditions. In other words, you must be ready to disregard pointings, verse divisions, and other markings whenever your exegetical judgment suggests that they are unreliable. Much more information on the Masoretic indicators is found in Würthwein's *The Text of the Old Testament* and in Danker's *Multipurpose Tools for Bible Study* (see III.1.b).

## 2. TRANSLATION

### 2.a. *Translation Theory*

A good translation not only renders the words of the original into their best English equivalents; it also reflects the style, the spirit, and even the impact of the original wherever possible. You are the best judge of what constitutes a faithful translation. Your familiarity with the passage in the original, and with the audience for whom you write or preach, allows you to choose your words to maximize the accuracy of the translation. Remember that accuracy does not require wooden literalism. The words of different languages do not correspond to one another on a one-for-one basis. Your translation should leave the same impression with you when you read it as does the original. A translation that meets this criterion can be considered faithful to the original.

Two recent books on Bible translation are very valuable. Both should be read in their entirety, rather than referred to only for specific information.

John Beekman and John Callow, *Translating the
   Word of God* (Zondervan Publishing House,
   1974).
This book contains serious, thoughtful discussions of
the special problems presented by translating Scripture
from one language to another. There is advice on how
to handle metaphors, similes, words with multiple
meanings, idioms, etc.

Sakae Kubo and Walter Specht, *So Many Versions?*
   (Zondervan Publishing House, 1975).
Kubo and Specht review at length the major twentieth-
century translations of the Bible, providing copious
examples from each, and commenting throughout on
the translation techniques and assumptions involved.

**2.b.  *Translation Aids***

Even if your knowledge of Hebrew, Greek, and
other languages has deteriorated (or was never adequate), you can still work profitably with the original
languages by using several English-oriented texts.
Don't hesitate to use these. There is no shame in saving
time and frustration, and no value in guessing your way
through material you simply can't read.

For the Hebrew OT there is a complete interlinear
edition available. It contains an acceptable translation
printed in interlinear fashion, as well as separately in
paragraph form alongside the main text. It is especially
useful for skimming through larger passages:

Jay P. Green (gen. ed.), *The Interlinear Bible: He-
   brew/English;* 3 vols. (Evansville, Ind.: Associated Publishers and Authors, 1976; repr.
   Baker Book House, 1979).
Also available for part of the OT is a similar interlinear edition, somewhat less useful because it is more
wooden in style:

Joseph Magil, *The Englishman's Linear Hebrew-*

*English Old Testament* (Zondervan Publishing House, 1974).

For the LXX no interlinear is available, but a convenient side-by-side Greek and English publication does exist:

*The Septuagint Version of the Old Testament with an English Translation* (London: Samuel Bagster & Sons, n.d.; repr. Zondervan Publishing House, 1970).

A translation of the Syriac Peshitta into English has been made. It is usually reliable, and serves to tell you when the Peshitta is different from the MT and other versions, even if you do not know Syriac well:

George M. Lamsa, *The Holy Bible from Ancient Eastern Manuscripts* (A. J. Holman Co., 1957).

Various portions of the Aramaic Targums are available in English translation. Among these are:

J. W. Etheridge, *The Targums of Onkelos and Jonathan ben Uzziel on the Pentateuch;* 2 vols. (London: Longman, Green, Longman and Roberts, 1862–1865).

Bernard Grossfeld (ed.), *The Targum to the Five Megilloth* (Hermon Press, 1973).

The Latin Vulgate is also translated into English:

Ronald Knox, *The Old Testament: Newly Translated from the Vulgate Latin;* 2 vols. (Sheed & Ward, 1948–1950).

Analytical lexicons list words directly as they occur in the biblical text, and then provide the parsing. They can be very useful as time-savers, but are not to be relied upon for meanings or other technical data. Use the formal lexicons for that purpose. For Hebrew and Aramaic there is:

Benjamin Davidson, *The Analytical Hebrew and Chaldee Lexicon* (London: Samuel Bagster & Sons, 1848; 2d ed. 1850; repr. Zondervan Publishing House, 1970).

For LXX Greek words, Bagster's analytical lexicon of the NT is often adequate even though its vocabulary is limited to words found in the NT:

> *The Analytical Greek Lexicon Revised,* ed. by Harold K. Moulton (originally published as *The Analytical Greek Lexicon;* London: Samuel Bagster & Sons, 1852; rev. ed. 1908; new rev. ed., Zondervan Publishing House, 1978).

To make it easier to use the still-popular Brown, Driver, and Briggs Hebrew Lexicon (see III.8.a), an index has been produced that lists the Hebrew words mostly in the order in which they occur in the chapters and verses of each book, with reference given to the appropriate entry in BDB. Of course, such an aid is necessary only if your Hebrew is weak enough to make parsing a problem:

> Bruce Einspahr, *Index to the Brown, Driver and Briggs Hebrew Lexicon* (Moody Press, 1976).

## 3. HISTORY

### 3.a. *General Chronology*

A very convenient brief sketch of the chronology of the ancient Near East including Israel, by Frank Moore Cross, Jr., is available in:

> William L. Langer (ed.), *An Encyclopedia of World History;* rev. ed. (Houghton Mifflin Co., 1964), pp. 27–50.

For a somewhat longer but still concise overview of Israel and the rest of the ancient Near East see also:

> Siegfried J. Schwantes, *A Short History of the Ancient Near East* (Baker Book House, 1965).

The difficult problem of synchronizing the biblical chronologies of the Israelite and Judean kings is best handled by Thiele, whose ingenious solutions have increasingly gained acceptance:

Edwin R. Thiele, *A Chronology of the Hebrew Kings* (Zondervan Publishing House, 1977).

### 3.b. *Israelite History*

Most histories are written to be studied in their entirety rather than consulted here and there for information about specific times or events. Several major Israelite histories exist, however, which are fairly well suited to both purposes.

The most widely used history, respected for its cautious, judicious, and thorough scholarship is:

John Bright, *A History of Israel,* 2d ed. (Westminster Press, 1972).

Especially welcome because it follows very closely the Old Testament ordering and subject matter rather than being more generally a "secular" history of Israel is:

Charles F. Pfeiffer, *Old Testament History* (Baker Book House, 1973).

Noth's history is considerably more skeptical of the accuracy of the biblical account, but nevertheless erudite and insightful:

Martin Noth, *The History of Israel,* rev. ed. (Harper & Brothers, 1960).

A massive and often controversial work is that of Kaufmann. His five-volume series is now being translated into English. His work takes nothing for granted, but attempts fresh, frequently provocative analyses at every point:

Yehezkel Kaufmann, *History of the Religion of Israel: From the Babylonian Captivity to the End of the Prophecy;* Vol. 4 (KTAV Publishing House, 1977).

The prestigious *Cambridge Ancient History* has produced a revised edition of Volumes I and II, which treat developments relevant to OT history down to about

1000 B.C. Many chapters of these are also available in fascicle form (1961–1968).

> *The Cambridge Ancient History,* Vol. I, Parts 1 and 2, 3d ed; Vol. II, Parts 1 and 2, 3d ed.; Plates to Vols. 1 and 2, 2d ed. (Cambridge University Press, 1971–1977).

### 3.c.  *Other Parts of the Ancient Near East*

From among the many fine historical works on various peoples and cultures in the biblical world, several major works may be recommended for their comprehensiveness and reliability.

For a general presentation of the data on ethnic and national groups mentioned in the OT as Israel's neighbors or conquerors, see:

> Donald J. Wiseman (ed.), *Peoples of Old Testament Times* (Oxford University Press, 1973).

On Egyptian history the standard work is:

> Alan Gardiner, *Egypt of the Pharaohs* (1964; reprinted with corrections, Oxford University Press, 1966).

Specifically for the culture and religion of the Egyptians, including a sensitive analysis of the Egyptian mythopoeic (myth-making) religious mind, use:

> Henri Frankfort, *Ancient Egyptian Religion* (Harper & Row, Publishers, Harper Torchbooks, 1961).

A superb general survey of the literature, life, religion, and civil institutions of the ancient Sumerians, Babylonians, and Assyrians is found in:

> A. Leo Oppenheim, *Ancient Mesopotamia;* rev. ed. (University of Chicago Press, 1976).

Increased interest in Sumerian history and culture has resulted from the extraordinary new finds at Syrian Ebla. There is an especially readable introduction to Sumerian literature, especially to some documents with biblical parallels, in:

Samuel N. Kramer, *History Begins at Sumer* (Doubleday & Co., Anchor Books, 1959).

The Hittites exerted considerable early influence on Bible lands, even though they are not specifically mentioned in the Bible. (The "Hittites" of the Bible are the sons of Heth, a Canaanite group). The standard introduction to their history and civilization is:

O. R. Gurney, *The Hittites;* 2d ed. (Penguin Books, 1954).

For Persia, the best single history (with helpful indexes) remains:

A. T. Olmstead, *History of the Persian Empire* (University of Chicago Press, 1948).

## 3.d. *Archaeology*

Three introductions to the field of Palestinian archaeology are widely used, and there are also a variety of valuable sources available for specific knowledge about individual areas and sites. Unfortunately, many archaeologists either do not publish their excavation results at all, or else publish them in such a narrow, technical way that the average OT student cannot make reasonable use of them in exegesis, except as the excavation reports themselves draw attention to biblical texts.

The most popular introduction remains:

G. Ernest Wright, *Biblical Archaeology;* rev. and enl. ed. (Westminster Press, 1963).

Equally valuable and erudite is:

William F. Albright, *The Archaeology of Palestine;* rev. ed. (Penguin Books, 1960; repr. Peter Smith Publisher).

A survey with special attention to Jericho, Megiddo, and similar key sites is:

Kathleen Kenyon, *Archaeology in the Holy Land;* 2d ed. (Frederick A. Praeger, 1965).

A recent book by the same author emphasizes the latest findings:

Kathleen Kenyon, *The Bible and Recent Archaeology* (John Knox Press, 1978).

For a collection of maps, illustrations, and generally reliable commentary on the relationship of archaeological discoveries to OT history, particularly as related to specific books and even passages, consult:

Gaalyahu, Cornfeld, *Archaeology of the Bible: Book by Book;* David Noel Freedman, consulting ed. (Harper & Row, Publishers, 1976).

A systematic grouping of various topics and categories may be found in the very helpful work:

Michael Avi-Yonah (ed.), *Encyclopedia of Archaeological Excavations in the Holy Land;* 4 vols. (Prentice-Hall, 1975).

For an extensive review of the actual literary and historical sources of the ancient world from which archaeological information comes, see:

D. Winton Thomas (ed.), *Archaeology and Old Testament Study* (Oxford University Press, 1967).

It contains a lengthy Scripture index that allows you to locate quickly any data from ancient sources that may relate to your passage or book.

Finally, a large number of individual articles on key subjects and findings related to the OT have been gathered together in:

Edward F. Campbell, Jr., David Noel Freedman, and G. Ernest Wright (eds.), *The Biblical Archaeologist Reader;* 3 vols. (Doubleday & Co., 1961–1970).

### 3.e.  *Geographies and Atlases*

Two fine, authoritative studies on Holy Land geography (weather, agriculture, topography, etc.) may be used with much profit:

Denis Baly, *The Geography of the Bible* (Harper & Brothers, 1957).

Yohanan Aharoni, *The Land of the Bible: A Historical Geography*; rev. and enl. ed. (Westminster Press, 1980).

The best atlas for OT studies is also the easiest to use, and the most helpful in exegetical tasks. It is chock full of maps, charts, and other illustrations, accompanied by clear explanatory notes. The many biblical passages to which the atlas is relevant are contained in a separate index, as well as with each illustration:

Yohanan Aharoni and Michael Avi-Yonah (eds.), *The Macmillan Bible Atlas* (Macmillan Co., 1968; rev. ed. 1977).

Next best is the widely used, though aging:

G. Ernest Wright and Floyd V. Filson, *The Westminster Historical Atlas to the Bible;* rev. ed. (Westminster Press, 1956).

Four other reliable atlases give excellent coverage and are widely available:

Denis Baly and A. D. Tushingham, *Atlas of the Biblical World* (World Publishing Co., 1971).

Emil G. Kraeling, *Rand McNally Bible Atlas* (Rand McNally & Co., 1956).

Herbert G. May et al. (eds.), *Oxford Bible Atlas;* 2d ed. (Oxford University Press, 1974).

J. H. Negenman, *New Atlas of the Bible,* ed. by H. H. Rowley (Doubleday & Co., 1969).

## 3.f. *Historical Criticism*

As it is most narrowly defined, historical criticism is concerned with the historical settings of biblical texts, including the establishing of names, dates, and times for events mentioned or attended to in a given passage. The aim of this sort of historical criticism is to arrive at a useful understanding of the relevant historical factors, in a form that elucidates them fully. Thus the historian goes well beyond the limits of the passage itself in establishing the historical factors and trends, more or less independently of the way they happen to be presented in the Bible.

However, historical criticism is a term also used to mean what is otherwise called the historical-critical method. This method has as its basic assumption the idea that "objective" biblical-historical study must treat the Bible like any other book, putting aside such "subjective" ideas as inspiration, authority, divine causation, etc. For obvious reasons, the historical-critical method is a subject of great debate as to its own "objectivity."

A lucid introduction to the special issues involved and the methodological assumptions is:

> Edgar Krentz, *The Historical-Critical Method;* Guides to Biblical Scholarship (Fortress Press, 1975).

A properly motivated but inadequately documented attack on the historical-critical method may be found in:

> Gerhard Maier, *The End of the Historical-Critical Method* (Concordia Publishing House, 1977).

Very helpful as a corrective to the kind of unchecked skepticism that has characterized some OT historical studies in the name of objectivity is:

> Kenneth A. Kitchen, *Ancient Orient and Old Testament* (London: Inter-Varsity Fellowship, Tyndale Press, 1966).

For a review of some of the difficulties encountered in the historical study of the OT, see:

> J. Maxwell Miller, *The Old Testament and the Historian;* Guides to Biblical Scholarship (Fortress Press, 1976).

**3.g.** *Tradition Criticism*

The study of the history of oral traditions as they functioned to preserve the literature and especially the history of ancient Israel before formalization in writing is called tradition criticism.

Two fine introductions to this somewhat theoretical field are:

> Douglas A. Knight, *Rediscovering the Traditions of Israel* (Scholars Press and the Society of Biblical Literature, 1973).

> Walter Rast, *Tradition History and the Old Testament;* Guides to Biblical Scholarship (Fortress Press, 1972).

## 4. LITERARY ANALYSIS

**4.a.** *Parallel Literature*

The Bible is a unique book; there is nothing like it. There are, however, many individual literary works preserved from the ancient world which are remarkably similar to *parts* of the Bible. To ignore these valuable parallels where they exist is to impoverish an exegesis. Fortunately, the majority of the known parallels have been collected for easy reference.

The most complete, massive translation of (usually complete) texts parallel to the OT is found in the following edition, which is recommended even though very expensive:

> James B. Pritchard (ed.), *Ancient Near Eastern Texts Relating to the Old Testament;* 3d ed. with supplement (Princeton University Press, 1969).

Two abridgements are found in:

> James B. Pritchard (ed.), *The Ancient Near East: An Anthology of Texts and Pictures* (Princeton University Press, 1958); Vol. II: *The Ancient Near*

*East: A New Anthology of Texts and Pictures*
(Princeton University Press, 1976).

Both the full edition and the abridgements contain indexes of Scripture references for easy correlation to biblical passages. (The companion volumes of pictures are listed at III.11.f.)

Much of the time, your interest will probably be focused toward parallel literature from the ancient Near East which is specifically religious in nature. A thorough, well-documented collection of the strictly religious texts pertaining to the OT has been published. It contains more comprehensive introductions and generally more helpful notes than Pritchard's volume, and is just as complete with regard to the religious documents:

> Walter Beyerlin (ed.), *Near Eastern Religious Texts Relating to the Old Testament;* The Old Testament Library (Westminster Press, 1978).

For the very important individual semantic parallels from the many Late Bronze Age tablets found at Ugarit, there is a very useful collection built around words, terms, and concepts that occur in both Ugaritic and Hebrew. These include animals, plants, numerals, names, professions, social institutions, literary phrases, literary genres, etc.:

> Loren Fisher (ed.), *Ras Shamra Parallels: The Texts from Ugarit and the Hebrew Bible;* 2 vols.; Analecta Orientalia 49, 50 (Rome: Pontifical Biblical Institute, 1972, 1976).

Each entry has a translation of the Ugaritic passage, textual notes, a bibliography, and an evaluation of the Ugaritic-Hebrew connections.

You can learn much about the beliefs of the Canaanites, so important in OT times, by reading for yourself their major myths. The best translation of these is by Coogan:

> Michael Coogan, *Stories from Ancient Canaan* (Westminster Press, 1978).

**4.b.** *Genre Criticism*

The criticism or analysis of genres (literary types) is usually limited to larger literary units and styles such as law, history, wisdom. Often, however, individual scholars may use "genre" interchangeably with "form," so that there is no distinction between form criticism (see III.5.a) and genre criticism, and thus no distinction between larger literary types (genres) and smaller, specific individual types (forms). Even though the distinction between the two types may be considered somewhat arbitrary, and even though it is a subjective decision as to whether a given literary type is general and large enough to be a genre or small and specific enough to be a form, the distinction is still useful and it is recommended that you follow it. Thus, for example, "narrative" is considered a whole genre, but a "census narrative" would be considered an individual form; "wisdom" is a whole genre, but a "numerical wisdom enumeration" would be considered a specific form; elegiac poetry might be frequent enough in the OT to be called a genre, whereas a "battle aftermath lament" such as II Sam. 1:19–27 would be specific enough to be considered a "form." As a rule, you should confine use of the term "genre" to literary types that are represented fairly widely by varying subtypes; the subtypes themselves are the forms.

The best overall introduction to genres (and forms as well) is found in Eissfeldt's *The Old Testament: An Introduction* (III.1.b), Part One.

**4.c.** *Redaction Criticism*

Redaction criticism concerns itself with how the various units that comprise a section or book of the OT were put together in their intermediate or final form. It therefore requires analysis of the work of the (anonymous) editors of the section or book, and is accordingly a very speculative kind of criticism since nothing is directly known about editorial activity or the editors themselves.

An introduction to the subject has been written by Perrin, which, however, concentrates largely on the NT rather than the OT:

> Norman Perrin, *What Is Redaction Criticism?* Guides to Biblical Scholarship (Fortress Press, 1969).

### 4.d.  *Literary Criticism*

There are several ways in which the term "literary criticism" is used. For many years, literary criticism meant little more than source criticism (e, below). Occasionally it meant roughly what the term historical criticism is now used to describe (see III.3.f). Increasingly, however, the term is used in its most basic meaning to refer to the process of analyzing and understanding parts of the Bible as literature, examining technique, style, and other features in order to gain an appreciation for the intention and results of a given portion as a literary composition. As an introduction, with somewhat controversial examples of the method applied, see:

> David Robertson, *The Old Testament and the Literary Critic;* Guides to Biblical Scholarship (Fortress Press, 1977).

### 4.e.  *Source Criticism*

Applicable mostly in the case of the Pentateuch, and to a lesser extent the historical books, source criticism attempted to discern the various written documents which the final editor (of the Pentateuch, for example) drew from in producing the finished work. This criticism is now considered outdated since the human "sources" of the OT are far more complex and more difficult to recover or isolate than a few written documents would be. Even so, the general features of the documentary hypothesis of Graf and Wellhausen, which posits four main sources for the Pentateuch (J, E, D, P) and suggests approximate dates for each, are still accepted by many OT scholars. An introduction to source criticism (under its alternate appellation, literary criticism) is found in:

> Norman C. Habel, *Literary Criticism of the Old Testament;* Guides to Biblical Scholarship (Fortress Press, 1971).

### 4.f. *Dating*

For many years the tendency among OT scholars was to date portions of Scripture on the basis of naive theories about the evolution of Israelite religion rather than on any intrinsic, objective criteria. The law was therefore dated late because it supposedly evidenced "developed" features, whereas the more "primitive" stories about Yahweh's leadership of the exodus, for example, could be dated early. Such hypothetical constructions are now largely out of favor, but great diversity still exists concerning the dating of various OT books and sections thereof. Dating books on the basis of linguistic features has always been inherently more objective in intent, but has suffered from a lack of specific knowledge. For poetry, there are some tentative approaches that would appear to offer hope. If your passage is poetry, you may be able to suggest a date for it—even if the context gives no clue—by consulting:

> David A. Robertson, *Linguistic Evidence in Dating Early Hebrew Poetry* (Scholars Press, 1973).

Robertson provides a preliminary typology for dating poetry according to mostly morphological features.

Also helpful is Chapter 1 of:
W. F. Albright, *Yahweh and the Gods of Canaan*
(Doubleday & Co., 1968).

In the case of a great deal of poetry, and virtually all prose, there is very little agreed-upon evidence that allows for specific dating on the basis of linguistic features. You must rely primarily on the claims of the text itself and nonlinguistic features. Orthographic (spelling) features in a few cases may be indicative of date. See:

Frank Moore Cross, Jr., and David Noel Freedman, *Early Hebrew Orthography* (American Oriental Society, 1952).

But in most cases, the orthography of the Hebrew OT is of no help; early and late texts alike are written in the orthography of the Persian period (540–333 B.C.), since the texts from early times were conjoined and copied widely during the Restoration. Thus a single orthography was applied through the entire OT in both Hebrew and Aramaic. Only the small portions that partially escape this leveling process (such as some of the earliest poems) can be dated by the orthographic evidence.

## 5. FORM

### 5.a. *Form Criticism*

The concern of form criticism is the isolation and analysis of specific literary types contained in a passage. From such an analysis the exegete can often discern something about the way the passage has been composed, its themes, its central interests, or even the type of situation in which it may have been employed (depending on the form) in ancient Israel. All of these bits of information may possibly be deduced even if the context of the passage itself does not contain them, because study of all the various manifestations of the specific form throughout the Bible (and other ancient literature where it exists) allows certain generalizations to be applied to each usage.

Of late, form criticism has come under attack as a method that yields too little "meaning" from passages, and one that neglects other valid critical techniques. Form criticism has also earned something of a bad name by being applied by some scholars in an all-encompassing manner, and with an overconfidence in the insights it can provide. For example, some form-critical enthusiasts have used the technique to arrive at firm conclusions about the dating, authorship, genuineness, originality, contextual propriety, historical validity, etc., of biblical passages, which the method in reality simply cannot support. It is more widely understood now that ancient writers (including the prophets, in whose books form criticism is especially employed) borrowed forms from the ancient world in a tentative manner and reworked them. Their own inspired creativity was everywhere evident, and they were hardly slaves to a set of rules to which the forms (and parts of forms) they used could always be conformed. Ancient biblical writers and speakers thus took what they wanted from the existing forms (the typical) and produced new combinations or constructions (the unique).

Two excellent sources for understanding form criticism are available. The best single introduction to the method is that of Tucker, who treats it systematically according to four elements: structure, genre, setting, and intention:

> Gene M. Tucker, *Form Criticism of the Old Testament;* Guides to Biblical Scholarship (Fortress Press, 1971).

A recent collection of six essays explains the history of, as well as current trends in, form criticism. For

understanding its goals and presuppositions, as well as
how it applies in various OT passages, see:

>   John H. Hayes (ed.), *Old Testament Form Criticism*
>   (Trinity University Press, 1974).

On the specific relationship of literary form to history, with instructive examples, see:

>   Martin J. Buss (ed.), *Encounter with the Text: Form
>   and History in the Hebrew Bible* (Fortress Press,
>   1979).

### 5.b.  *The Relationship of Form to Structure*

There is no way to discover a literary form or to
identify it properly without first identifying the various
items of which it is composed (its content) and the way
that those items are arranged in relation to one another
and in relation to the larger context (the structure). In
other words, the exegete faces the danger of putting the
cart before the horse if he or she jumps too quickly to
the conclusion that a passage contains, or is composed
in the manner of, form X, simply on the basis of some
key words that form X usually contains, or some other
stylistic features normally associated with form X. One
can actually go so far as to ignore the majority of the
evidence for form typology and mistakenly categorize
a form. Alternatively, one can place so much emphasis
on a strictly form-critical methodology that many exegetically significant features not contained in the results of the form-critical analysis are simply forgotten.

First, then, be sure that you understand the elements
of content and understand at least tentatively how the
elements are structured, before identifying a form. The
proper identification of the form(s) may subsequently
help you to refine your identification of the elements
and the structure; but don't let the known *typical* features of the form dominate the way you analyze the
*specific* features of the passage. Rather, it is just the

other way around: The specific features of the passage
tell you how much or how little any forms which happen to be present influence the passage, if at all—and
to what extent the form is pure, adapted, "broken," or
incomplete.

## 6. STRUCTURE

### 6.a. *Definitions*

At the present time five similar terms are used in OT
studies with varying degrees of frequency and with at
least two very different meanings. Three of these terms,
*structuralism, structural exegesis,* and *structural analy-*
*sis,* usually are employed to refer to a rather new kind
of linguistic analysis as applied to biblical studies.
Structuralism (the most common of these terms) is
concerned largely with certain special, rather technically defined, relationships between or within the words
in a sentence. The structuralist seeks to understand the
rules by which language functions, on the theory that
those rules can lead to a deeper understanding of the
structure (and meaning) of the component parts of
sentences and of sentences themselves. Three recent
books explain structuralism and provide some examples of its use in biblical sentences:

Roland Barthes et al., *Structural Analysis and Bibli-*
   *cal Exegesis: Interpretational Essays* (Pickwick
   Press, 1974).
Jean Calloud, *Structural Analysis of Narrative* (For-
   tress Press and Scholars Press, 1976).
Daniel Patte and Aline Patte, *Structural Exegesis:*
   *From Theory to Practice* (Fortress Press, 1978).
Best for the beginner to learn from, however, is:
Daniel Patte, *What Is Structural Exegesis?* Guides
   to Biblical Scholarship (Fortress Press, 1976).
Two other terms, *structural criticism* and *structural*

*studies,* are usually employed to describe the way that larger units of text (passages) are composed of their various elements of content. The latter two terms, in other words, refer generally to the content structure of a passage, whereas the former three terms refer to concern for the linguistic patterns in sentences.

Structuralism (the specialized linguistic analysis) is technical and narrowly applied, and is also rather devoid of interest in the historical, cultural, or theological, except in a secondary way. Thus it is not likely that you will find occasion to use it widely in any given exegesis. Like linguistic analysis in philosophy, the results are occasionally stellar, but too often meager. Nevertheless, the diligent student may find the task well worth the effort in particular passages.

For an understanding of the broader method of structural studies, how passages are put together from their constituent elements, how their structure may be deduced and outlined, and the significance for exegesis, there is a very fine, short book, filled with helpful examples:

Robert C. Culley, *Studies in the Structure of Hebrew Narrative* (Fortress Press and Scholars Press, 1976).

The broader method of structural studies is far more likely to be of constant value to exegetes, as is the broader discipline of rhetorical criticism whose methods may in one sense be considered to encompass structural studies as well.

### 6.b.  *Rhetorical Criticism*

Rhetorical criticism is concerned with how a literary unit (usually a passage) is put together. Whereas form criticism tends to emphasize the typical and general, rhetorical criticism concentrates on the genius of a passage—that which is personal, specific, unique, or original. The rhetorical critic seeks to understand the inspired writer's logic, style, and purpose. To do this, emphasis must be placed on (a) the patterns found within the literary unit; (b) the individual stylistic devices that contribute to the overall impact of the whole unit; and (c) the relationship of the parts to the whole. Rhetorical criticism is most often synchronic (concerned with the passage as it stands now) rather than diachronic (concerned with the theoretical history of how the passage might have been transmitted, mutated, reshaped, or edited before reaching its present form).

As currently practiced, rhetorical criticism emphasizes the structure of the canonical text, yet uses the most modern, reliable techniques to implement this emphasis. For the original statement of the need to go beyond the limits of form criticism to rhetorical criticism, see:

James Muilenburg, "Form Criticism and Beyond" (*Journal of Biblical Literature* 88 [1969], 1–18).

A number of excellent examples of rhetorical criticism applied to various biblical passages are found in:

Jared J. Jackson and Martin Kessler (eds.), *Rhetorical Criticism: Essays in Honor of James Muilenburg* (Pickwick Press, 1974).

### 6.c. *Formula Criticism*

Certain groups of words (sometimes individual words) tend to appear in different passages in similar ways. When a word group functions consistently to express a given essential idea, yet in a variety of contexts, it is called a formula. Poetry seems to have many more formulae than does prose. Some examples (in translation) of common, well-known formulae are: "I will bless thy name"; "Lord of Hosts"; "Great is the Lord and greatly to be praised"; etc. Such formulae appear in a variety of passages. To understand how formulae function, how they represent "building blocks" within literary units, how they relate to the meter of a passage, etc., is the goal of formula criticism. Because formula criticism emphasizes the comparison of formula contexts, it is especially relevant to biblical context (step 9) and to structure (step 6). Two fine books explain the process and its implications for exegesis:

> Robert C. Culley, *Oral Formulaic Language in the Biblical Psalms* (University of Toronto Press, 1967).
> William R. Watters, *Formula Criticism and the Poetry of the Old Testament* (Berlin and New York: Walter de Gruyter, 1976).

**6.d.** *Poetry Analysis (Poetics)*

Poetics is a vast study. Nevertheless, a proper feel for the poetry of the OT is not so hard to come by that it should be avoided. In fact, with a reasonable investment of time the student of the OT can move rather quickly from relative ignorance to relative competence in analyzing poetry. It is especially important to be able to recognize the types of parallelism and the metrical structure which characterize a given passage of poetry, and good sources are available for each.

For a brief but clear introduction to both issues, see:

> Norman K. Gottwald, "Poetry, Hebrew" in *The Interpreter's Dictionary of the Bible* (Abingdon Press, 1972), Vol. III, pp. 829–838.

For a more comprehensive coverage, see:

> George Buchanan Gray, *The Forms of Hebrew Poetry,* with Prolegomenon by David Noel Freedman (KTAV Publishing House, 1970).

In order to analyze certain types of poetic parallelism effectively, you will need to learn how "fixed pairs" of words function in OT poems. The best (and clearest)

introduction to this analysis, with hundreds of easy-to-
follow examples is:

Stanley Gevirtz, *Patterns in the Early Poetry of Israel* (University of Chicago Press, 1964).

On Hebrew meter, see:

Douglas K. Stuart, *Studies in Early Hebrew Meter*
(Scholars Press and Harvard Semitic Museum,
1976).

The situation as regards meter is more difficult for
the student, since conflicting theories of metrical composition still persist. Nevertheless, whichever of the
four most common approaches ("stress" meter, semantic parallelism meter; alternating meter, syllabic meter)
is used, if used consistently it will provide the student
with an objective means of discerning and evaluating
the relative length of lines of poetry and also the way
that lines may be grouped together into couplets and
triplets (often called bicola and tricola), or large units
(sometimes called strophes).

## 7. GRAMMAR

### 7.a. *Reference Grammars*

Properly used, the reference grammars are a ready
source of exegetically relevant information. The grammars often collect together many or all of the instances
of a certain type of grammatical phenomenon. When
you refer to the grammar for information on such a
phenomenon, you are thus provided with a list of parallels and an explanation of how the phenomenon functions in the OT. That can be just the sort of information
you need to help you make certain exegetical decisions.

For Hebrew the standard reference grammar is:

F. W. Gesenius, *Hebrew Grammar,* rev. by E.
Kautzsch; 2d English ed., ed. and tr. by A. E.
Cowley (Oxford: Clarendon Press, 1910).

The most sophisticated of the introductory grammars is:

Thomas O. Lambdin, *Introduction to Biblical Hebrew* (Charles Scribner's Sons, 1971).

Outstanding for its collection of instances of grammatical features from throughout the Hebrew Bible, and for its brilliant solutions for many problematic grammatical issues is:

Alexander Sperber, *A Historical Grammar of Biblical Hebrew* (Leiden: E. J. Brill, 1966).

For Aramaic grammatical features, you will probably find everything you need in the concise but very reliable:

Franz Rosenthal, *A Grammar of Biblical Aramaic* (Wiesbaden: Otto Harrassowitz, 1961).

If you wish to refer to data relevant to Aramaic grammar from the entire Old Aramaic period (earliest texts through the end of the Persian empire in 333 B.C., a massive, technical, very comprehensive source is:

Stanislav Segert, *Altaramäische Grammatik* (Leipzig: Verlag Enzyklopädie, VEB, 1975).

An excellent grammar for the Septuagint has long been available:

Henry St. J. Thackeray, *A Grammar of the Old Testament in Greek According to the Septuagint* (Cambridge University Press, 1909).

If you do exegesis of passages of poetry, especially the Psalms or Job, you may find in the secondary literature frequent reference to two languages, Ugaritic and Phoenician, which are very similar to Hebrew. Even if you have not studied these languages formally, you may be able to understand something of their relevance and helpfulness on specific points by consulting the following grammars:

Cyrus H. Gordon, *Ugaritic Textbook* (Rome: Pontifical Biblical Institute, 1965).

Zellig S. Harris, *A Grammar of the Phoenician Language* (American Oriental Society, 1936).

Stanislav Segert, *A Grammar of Phoenician and Punic* (Munich: C. H. Beck, 1976).

## 7.b. *Other Technical Sources*

It is sometimes helpful to be able to refer to a comparative grammar, one that groups Hebrew forms and features in the context of those of other Semitic languages. The standard is considered:

Sabatino Moscati (ed.), *An Introduction to the Comparative Grammar of the Semitic Languages: Phonology and Morphology* (Wiesbaden: Otto Harrassowitz, 1964).

In order to understand Hebrew in the more immediate context of the Canaanite language family, see both of the following:

Zellig S. Harris, *Development of the Canaanite Dialects* (American Oriental Society, 1939).

William L. Moran, "The Hebrew Language in Its Northwest Semitic Background," in G. Ernest Wright (ed.), *The Bible and the Ancient Near East* (Doubleday & Co., 1961).

Orthography (spelling analysis) is a technical study within the field of grammar which can occasionally help the exegete unravel aspects of a difficult text. The standard study compares Hebrew with Phoenician, Aramaic, and Moabite during the OT period, based on the evidence of the inscriptions dating to OT times:

Frank Moore Cross, Jr., and David Noel Freedman, *Early Hebrew Orthography* (American Oriental Society, 1952).

## 8. LEXICAL ANALYSIS

### 8.a. *Lexicons*

A lexicon is a dictionary. The fact that the term "lexicon" has been used instead of the term "dictionary" by biblical and classical scholars is simply a quirk of linguistic history, well deserving of a word study of its own.

The lexicons are valuable sources of information about the words they list. Lexicons often devote lengthy articles (mini word studies) to those words which are especially interesting or significant theologically, and also to words that have any unusual or crucial features. It is a mistake to launch upon a word study or even to comment at length about the usage of a word in Scripture without first consulting the relevant lexicons.

The Hebrew lexicon to use (if possible) is:

Ludwig Koehler and Walter Baumgartner, *Lexicon in Veteris Testamenti Libros;* 2d ed. (Leiden: E. J. Brill, 1958).

This lexicon is the world's standard. It is in the process of revision, under a new name *(Hebräisches und aramäisches Lexicon zum Alten Testament,* ed. by B. Hartmann, P. Reymond, J. J. Stamm; 3d ed.; Fascicle II, ṭbḥ-nbṭ; Leiden: E. J. Brill, 1974). The 2d (1958) edition has both German (good) and English (sometimes imperfect) definitions. The 3d (1974ff.) edition has only German. If you cannot read German, see Holladay's lexicon:

William L. Holladay, *A Concise Hebrew and Aramaic Lexicon of the Old Testament* (Wm. B. Eerdmans Publishing Co., 1971).

This lexicon is an English work based upon the Koehler-Baumgartner second edition (1958) and the two-thirds completed third edition manuscript. It is thus very much up-to-date and highly reliable. However, it does not contain the detailed and useful references to cognates in other Semitic languages that characterize the full articles of Koehler-Baumgartner and "BDB." The latter continues to be widely used:

> Francis Brown, S. R. Driver, Charles A. Briggs, *A Hebrew and English Lexicon of the Old Testament* (Oxford: Clarendon Press, 1907; repr. 1962, 1966).

BDB is still very useful because of the sheer volume of its fine articles, though it is somewhat outdated because it lacks cognate information from Ugaritic and other recent finds. The suggested etymologies (histories of word origins and their relation to Semitic word roots) are often unacceptable.

For Aramaic, the standard source in English is:

> Marcus Jastrow, *A Dictionary of the Targumim, the Talmud Babli and Yerushalmi, and the Midrashic Literature;* 2 vols; 2d ed. (1926; repr. New York: Pardes Publishing House, 1950).

A grammar such as Rosenthal's (III.7.a) also functions as a lexicon to some extent.

If you can read Latin, the best Aramaic lexicon of all is yours to use:

> Ernesto Vogt, *Lexicon Linguae Aramaicae Veteris Testamenti Documentis Antiquis Illustratum* (Rome: Pontifical Biblical Institute, 1971).

For the Septuagint, nothing excels:

> Henry G. Liddell and Robert Scott, *A Greek-English Lexicon,* rev. by Henry Stuart Jones and Roderick McKenzie; 9th ed. (Oxford: Clarendon Press, 1940).

See also:

> E. A. Barber et al. (eds.), *Supplement to A Greek-English Lexicon* (Oxford University Press, 1968).

For working from the Syriac Peshitta, use:

R. Payne Smith, *A Compendious Syriac Dictionary,*
    ed. by J. Payne Smith (Oxford: Clarendon Press,
    1903; repr. 1957).

The massive *Latin Dictionary* of Lewis and Short is
excellent for the Vulgate and other Latin texts:

Charlton T. Lewis and Charles Short, *A Latin Dic-
    tionary* [also titled *A New Latin Dictionary;* first
    published as *Harper's Latin Dictionary;* founded
    on Andrews' edition of Freund's Latin Dictio-
    nary] (New York, 1879; repr. Oxford University
    Press).

Since much lexical information about OT Hebrew
has come from Assyrian/Babylonian and Ugaritic
sources, from time to time you may find it necessary to
consult the lexicons for these languages.

For Assyrian/Babylonian, use wherever possible the
still incomplete:

Ignace Gelb, Benno Landsberger, A. Leo Oppen-
    heim, Erika Reiner, et al. (eds.), *The Chicago As-
    syrian Dictionary* (Oriental Institute of the Uni-
    versity of Chicago, 1956– ).

For those who can read German, von Soden's dictionary is excellent:

Wolfram von Soden, *Akkadisches Handwörterbuch*
    (Wiesbaden: Otto Harrassowitz, 1965).

For Ugaritic words, the only comprehensive lexicon
is in German:

Joseph Aisleitner, *Wörterbuch der ugaritischen
    Sprache;* 4th ed. (Berlin: Akademie-Verlag,
    1974).

An up-to-date Phoenician-Punic lexicon is now
available:

Richard Tomback, *A Comparative Semitic Lexicon
    of the Phoenician and Punic Languages* (Scholars
    Press, 1978).

## 8.b. Concordances

A concordance lists the places where a given word occurs throughout the Bible (or some other literary collection). Concordances can help you determine the usage, distribution, and contextualizations of any given word (see below, 8.c) and are thus one of the most valuable tools for lexical analysis. It is almost impossible to do word studies without concordances, and almost impossible to do thorough exegesis without word studies.

The standard, most comprehensive concondance is Mandelkern's. It is written in Latin and Hebrew only, and lists words in a somewhat complicated order (partly by context within a given book rather than by successive references) but these drawbacks are minor:

Solomon Mandelkern, *Veteris Testamenti Concordantiae Hebraicae atque Chaldaicae;* 8th ed. (Jerusalem: Schocken Books, 1969).

A somewhat easier-to-use although less complete concordance is:

Gerhard Lisowsky, *Konkordanz zum hebräischen Alten Testament* (Stuttgart: Württembergische Bibelanstalt, 1958).

If your Hebrew is nonexistent or not good enough to follow the contexts printed in Hebrew in Mandelkern or Lisowsky, you should use a concordance that lists words according to the Hebrew but with an English (King James Version, as it happens) citation of the contexts. Best for this purpose is:

George V. Wigram, *The Englishman's Hebrew and Chaldee Concordance of the Old Testament* (London: Samuel Bagster & Sons; 3d ed. 1874; repr. Zondervan Publishing House, 1978).

Yielding virtually the same information although in a more roundabout format (thus requiring more steps to follow the listings of a single Hebrew word) is:

Robert Young, *Analytical Concordance to the Bible;* 22d American ed. (Funk & Wagnalls Co., 1955).

For the Septuagint, a complete concordance exists. In analyzing the text of a passage you must analyze the Septuagint wording. The only way to know whether the Septuagint wordings are unique, unusual, or common is to consult the concordance, which gives the Hebrew word equivalents for the Greek word chosen by the Septuagint translators.

Edwin Hatch and Henry A. Redpath, *A Concordance to the Septuagint and the Other Greek Versions of the Old Testament;* 3d ed.; 2 vols. (Graz: Akademische Druck & Verlagsanstalt, 1955).

There also exists a brief but very useful (and inexpensive) one-volume Septuagint concordance:

George Morrish, *A Concordance of the Septuagint* (London: Samuel Bagster & Sons; repr. Zondervan Publishing House, 1976).

There are also special concordances to Qumran texts, to parts of the Targum, to some individual OT books, to certain ancient writers, etc. Marrow's *Basic Tools* (see Introduction, above) contains ample bibliographical data on such special concordances for those not infrequent occasions when you will find it necessary to pursue in detail a word's usage substantially beyond the biblical evidence. For the books of the Apocrypha a complete concordance now exists, keyed to English words but listing the Greek equivalents:

Lester T. Whitelocke (ed.), *An Analytical Concordance of the Books of the Apocrypha* (University Press of America, 1978).

### 8.c. *Word Studies*

A word study is a thorough analysis of the meaning(s) of a word, designed to arrive at its specific meaning in a given passage. There are various ways to approach a word study, but the following outline will serve as a basic guide. In any case, a word study seeks to establish how the word under investigation is used (1) in general; (2) in various contexts; (3) in the passage itself. The steps to establish this are:

1. Using a concordance, find where all the OT occurrences of the word are. If the word is common, think in terms of groups of occurrences; if rare, you may be able to examine all the usages in detail. Because of the magnitude of the enterprise, you may find it advisable to set more narrow limits (e.g., "the meaning of *zānāh* in Hosea").

2. Using other aids such as lexicons, take cognizance of the non-OT usages of the word (in inscriptions, Rabbinic literature, etc.).

3. Using lexicons, take note of any cognates in other languages you are able to work in.

4. Examine the biblical usage, trying to establish the various ranges of meaning that the word and its cognates seem to have.

5. Examine the distribution of the word. Much can be learned about the meaning this way. Is the word used only or mostly by the prophets, for example? That might tell you a great deal about its meaning. Is it used only or mostly in legal formulas? In certain kinds of expressions? Look for patterns wherever possible.

6. Establish the key usages—those which are unambiguous enough that they really pin down the word's meaning in a definitive way.

7. Center on the word's function in the passage itself. Bring all you have learned in the word study so far to bear on the passage, relating the specific use and meaning in the passage to the ranges of use and meaning known from elsewhere.

8. Offer a paraphrase, synonyms, a summary statement, or all of these, to your reader or congregation as a means of defining the word. In other words, give your

own "dictionary" definition of the word, not just in its
general use or uses, but according to its use in the
passage itself.

### 8.d.  *Theological Dictionaries*

The theological dictionaries provide the reader
with the results of careful word studies. Obviously
they must limit themselves to the broad, general usage
of words and cannot usually focus on individual passages. But they are nevertheless invaluable as timesav-
ing, informative exegetical resources. It is important
not to accept blindly the conclusions of any theological dictionary article, however. A given writer's view
can be slanted unfairly. It is best to follow with a critical eye the arguments and the evidence contained in
the article.

The best OT theological dictionary is just beginning
to appear, containing words from only the first letters
of the Hebrew alphabet. It is thorough, erudite, and
invaluable as a reference tool:

> G. Johannes Botterweck and Helmer Ringgren
> (eds.), *Theological Dictionary of the Old Testa-
> ment;* Vols. 1–3; rev. ed. (Wm. B. Eerdmans Pub-
> lishing Co., 1974–1978). In progress.

Two other similar books, less technical and less exhaustive in their coverage, are very helpful in word
study:

> Johannes B. Bauer (ed.), *Encyclopedia of Biblical
> Theology;* 3 vols. (London: Sheed & Ward, 1970).
> Alan Richardson (ed.), *A Theological Word Book of
> the Bible* (London: SCM Press, 1950).

You can also use with great profit the major Bible
dictionaries, which contain detailed articles on hundreds of key words and terms. And the massive TDNT
has much background on OT terms with equivalents in
the NT:

> Gerhard Kittel and Gerhard Friedrich (eds.), *Theological Dictionary of the New Testament;* 10 vols. including index vol. (Wm. B. Eerdmans Publishing Co., 1964–1976).

## 8.e. *Inscriptions*

Reading and analyzing inscriptions is a specialty that requires linguistic and philological training beyond the interests of most students and pastors. Nevertheless, a detailed word study may well take you to the inscriptional evidence. If you can read French, you can follow the inscriptional evidence for Northwest Semitic words (and their roots) in:

> Charles-François Jean and Jacob Hoftijzer, *Dictionnaire des inscriptions sémitiques de l'ouest* (Leiden: E. J. Brill, 1965).

There are many fine analytical collections of inscriptions, in various languages, with varying contents. While many of the important inscriptions are translated in Pritchard's ANET (see III.4.a, above), their vocabulary is not analyzed there. Two English sources for inscriptional data are:

> John C. L. Gibson, *Textbook of Syrian Semitic Inscriptions:* Vol. I, *Hebrew and Moabite Inscriptions;* Vol. II, *Aramaic Inscriptions* (Oxford University Press, 1971, 1975).

> Walter Aufrecht and John C. Hurd, *A Synoptic Concordance of Aramaic Inscriptions* (Biblical Research Associates and Scholars Press, 1975).

The single most comprehensive source is in German:

> M. Donner and W. Röllig, *Kanaanäische und aramäische Inschriften;* 2d ed. (Wiesbaden: Otto Harrassowitz, 1966).

## 9. BIBLICAL CONTEXT

### 9.a.  *Chain Reference Lists*

Many Bible editions in English contain what is col-
loquially called a "chain" reference list. In a separate
column, or at the end of each verse, reference is given
to passages elsewhere in the Bible which are in some
way similar to or connected with that verse. None of
these reference lists is entirely reliable or consistent,
and many suggest references that are farfetched or un-
reasonable. Nevertheless, these lists can often lead you
quickly to parallel or related passages not necessarily
containing the same words found in the passage you are
working on, and thus not to be found by the use of a
concordance. Three Bible editions contain especially
ample reference lists:

> *The Thompson Chain Reference Bible* (Kirkbride
> Bible Co., 1964)—KJV.
> *Harper Study Bible* (Harper & Row, Publishers,
> 1964)—RSV.
> *New American Standard Bible,* Reference Edition
> (A. J. Holman Co., 1976)—NASB.

### 9.b.  *Topical Concordances*

Most students are familiar with word concordances
(see III.8.b). A word concordance can serve both to
facilitate word studies and to guide the student to biblical context data. For the latter purpose, the concordance is used as a quick means of searching the OT
(and NT) for: (1) parallel passages containing the word;
and (2) parallel passages containing related topics or
concepts which are found by reference to their characteristic vocabulary.

In addition to word concordances, however, there
are topical concordances, which group together biblical

passages related to one another by a common topic or theme. These can be immensely valuable in suggesting to you other passages related to the one you are working on. In a sense, the topical concordances do what the reference lists do, only in much more detail and usually with the entire text of related passages printed out for immediate analysis.

There are five prominent topical concordances, all of which are profitable. The standard is:

> Orville J. Nave, *Nave's Topical Bible* (Moody Press, 1974).

In most cases equally useful are:

> Roswell D. Hitchcock, *Baker's Topical Bible* (Baker Book House, 1952).
>
> Charles R. Joy, *Harper's Topical Concordance;* rev. and enl. ed. (Harper & Row, Publishers, 1976).
>
> Edward Viening (ed.), *The Zondervan Topical Bible* (Zondervan Publishing House, 1969).

One topical concordance lists ample references but does not print out the texts in full:

> *The Holman Topical Concordance* (A. J. Holman Co., 1973).

### 9.c. *Commentaries and Biblical Context*

One of the tasks of a commentator is to bring to the attention of the reader the manner in which a passage relates to the book in which it is found, and to the wider biblical context as well. The insights of a commentator usually go beyond what you can happen upon by using references and concordances. Therefore, it pays to consult several exegetically oriented commentaries, both classical and modern, looking specifically for indications of intrabiblical relationships. For specific bibliographical information on exegetical commentary series, see III.11.f.

**9.d.** *Apocrypha and Pseudepigrapha*

Ancient Judaism produced certain religious works that purported to be revelatory and were modeled on biblical writings. A fair number of these have survived, partly because they were accorded at least semiscriptural status by one group or another in the early centuries A.D. These are called respectively the Apocrypha ("obscure works") and the Pseudepigrapha (works falsely attributed to a given author). Though almost exclusively post-Old Testament in date, and though rejected from canonicity by Jewish and Christian councils (with the notable exception of the sixteenth-century Catholic formalization of the Apocrypha as canonical), these books are very closely related to parts of the OT and very useful to OT exegesis. Though neither inspired nor doctrinally reliable, they are useful for philological, topical, historical, and stylistic comparisons. In the sense of genre, they are "biblical" in their type, and thus suitable for comparative purposes. Whenever possible, therefore, you should pay attention to these noncanonical writings for the data they contain.

The master publication of the Apocrypha and Pseudepigrapha is that of Charles:

> R. H. Charles (ed.), *The Apocrypha and Pseudepigrapha of the Old Testament:* Vol. I, Apocrypha; Vol. II, Pseudepigrapha (Oxford: Clarendon Press, 1913).

For a more complete listing of the major publications of Apocrypha and Pseudepigrapha (including a few pseudepigraphic works not published by Charles and concordances for two of the writings), see the bibliography (pp. 69–72) in:

> Stanley B. Marrow, *Basic Tools for Biblical Exegesis* (Rome: Biblical Institute Press, 1976).

A fine recent introduction to Apocrypha and Pseudepigrapha, along with other works, is found in:

Leonhard Rost, *Judaism Outside the Hebrew Canon* (Abingdon Press, 1976).

### 9.e. *The Old Testament in the New*

A demanding task is the analysis of OT themes, doctrines, etc., as they are reflected in the NT. All too often, OT exegetes neglect the NT data on the grounds that these represent later interpretations, muddying the exegetical waters. Unless you would go so far as to reject NT inspiration and authority, however, you are bound in the final analysis to relate the OT passage to any NT uses or classifications of it. As a general introduction to the principles involved, see:

F. F. Bruce, *The New Testament Development of Old Testament Themes* (Wm. B. Eerdmans Publishing Co., 1969).

For a comprehensive list of NT citations and allusions to OT passages, consult the "Index of Quotations" at the back of either the Nestle or the American Bible Society edition of the Greek New Testament.

## 10. THEOLOGY

### 10.a. *Old Testament Theologies*

Because the major OT theologies attempt a broad coverage of books and passages, it is often possible to use them profitably for exegetical guidance in relating a passage to OT theology as a whole. However, there is a great diversity of outlook represented by the various theologies, so they must be used with great caution. The major theologies reflect a "liberal" perspective, thus tending toward assumptions that may downplay the significance or trustworthiness of given portions and passages of the OT in favor of others. Nevertheless, a recognition of these biases does not mean that the theologies cannot be profitably used. In fact, if your own passage is consistently slighted by the OT theologies or its issues are in your opinion ignored by them, it becomes precisely your responsibility to demonstrate whether or not the theologies are derelict in doing so. If the theologies are found wanting, the force of your observations exegetically is all the more significant.

The two most popular OT theologies are:

Walther Eichrodt, *Theology of the Old Testament;* 2 vols.; The Old Testament Library (Westminster Press, 1961, 1967).

Gerhard von Rad, *Old Testament Theology;* 2 vols. (Harper & Row, Publishers, 1962, 1965).

Four other major OT theologies can also be very handy to the exegete largely because of their breadth in coverage of the OT data:

Edmond Jacob, *Theology of the Old Testament* (Harper & Brothers, 1958).

Walter Kaiser, Jr., *Toward an Old Testament Theology* (Zondervan Publishing House, 1978).

James Muilenburg, *The Way of Israel: Biblical Faith and Ethics* (Harper & Row, Publishers, 1961).

Walther Zimmerli, *Old Testament Theology in Outline* (John Knox Press, 1978).

Zimmerli's book is conveniently organized by topic, thus being especially easy to consult quickly.

A fine, reliable, and inexpensive paperback is:

Gerhard Hasel, *Old Testament Theology;* rev. ed. (Wm. B. Eerdmans Publishing Co., 1975).

## 10.b. *Christian Theologies*

Obviously, a Christian theology will give substantial attention to issues beyond the OT and will address the OT data less directly than will an OT theology. This broader perspective is valid and necessary for an exegesis to be entirely balanced in its conclusions. A most important criterion for exegetical value in a Christian theology is that it be biblically based, in constant dialogue with the text. In addition to the famous major theologies of well-known theologians such as Barth and Brunner, several works stand out as keenly biblical in orientation. One of the best by reason of its careful attention to OT issues and themes is:

Geerhardus Vos, *Biblical Theology* (Wm. B. Eerdmans Publishing Co., 1948).

Also intensely scriptural in interest, readable, and remarkably comprehensive is:

Herman Bavinck, *Our Reasonable Faith* (Wm. B. Eerdmans Publishing Co., 1956; repr. Baker Book House, 1977).

Remarkably thorough is the lengthy series of titles under the general title *Studies in Dogmatics:*

G. C. Berkouwer, *Studies in Dogmatics;* 14 vols. (Wm. B. Eerdmans Publishing Co., 1952–1976).

A standard theology from a Wesleyan perspective is:

H. Orton Wiley, *Christian Theology;* 3 vols. (Beacon Hill Press, 1940).

Also very sensitive to biblical issues throughout its two volumes so far in print has been:

Helmut Thielicke, *The Evangelical Faith;* Vols. 1 and 2 (Wm. B. Eerdmans Publishing Co., 1974, 1977); (Vol. 3 in preparation).

## 11. SECONDARY LITERATURE

### 11.a. *Special Reference Sources*

Large numbers of valuable articles and books are published every year in the OT field. What if someone, somewhere, may once have written an article or a portion of a book dealing exegetically with your passage? It would be deplorable to ignore such a work if it could be readily attained. Especially if your exegesis is in-

tended as a term paper or other substantial assignment,
you could hardly afford not to consult a careful work
devoted specifically to your topic. Virtually all scholarly OT publications are tabulated yearly and listed
both by topic and by Scripture reference in each annual
addition of:

> *Elenchus Bibliographicus Biblicus;* Vols. 1–48
> (1920–1967) in *Biblica;* published separately,
> 1968– (Vol. 49– ).

The first forty-eight volumes appeared in the journal
*Biblica* as annual supplements. You should consult the
relevant section (there are twenty-two sections) and the
alphabetical index for books and articles on your passage and related topics, during the year of publication.
The index is not cumulative; you must look through
each edition for relevant works published that year. But
the time is well spent in most cases.

The *Book List* of the British Society for Old Testament Study is an annual publication listing OT books
produced each year since 1946. Its special value beyond
the *Elenchus* is that each book is given a mini-review,
by which you can gauge something of its potential for
your own research. (The *Elenchus* lists only the bibliographical information without comment.) The *Book
List* listings have also been published in collections as
follows:

> H. H. Rowley (ed.), *Eleven Years of Bible Bibliogra-
> phy* (1946–1956); (Falcon's Wing Press, 1957).
> G. W. Anderson (ed.), *A Decade of Bible Bibliogra-
> phy* (1957–1966); (Oxford: Basil Blackwell, Pub-
> lisher, 1967).
> P. R. Ackroyd (ed.), *Bible Bibliography 1967–1973:
> Old Testament* (Oxford: Basil Blackwell, Pub-
> lisher, 1974).

The current editor of the *Book List* is Prof. R. N.
Whybray. Copies may be ordered from: Dr. A. D. H.
Mays, Trinity College, Dublin, Ireland.

A relatively new journal is now offering the kind of review of periodical articles in OT studies that has long been needed. It provides brief abstracts (representative summaries, sometimes with analytical comments) of articles on OT subjects appearing in a wide variety of periodicals. From the abstracts, you can get a sense of whether or not an article might be relevant to your study (the articles are listed by category), before investing the energy of hunting up the article itself. Some major books are also abstracted. Address: *Old Testament Abstracts,* Catholic Biblical Association of America, c/o Catholic University, Washington, D.C. 20064.

## 11.b. *The Journals*

Dozens of periodicals regularly carry articles related generally to the OT and specifically to OT exegesis. At the risk of slighting some of the best, a selection of ten journals is here recommended for their special attention to exegesis and exegetically important issues. The ten would likely be carried by most seminary libraries, and by many college and university libraries as well. If you make it a habit to pay attention to these journals, you will be rewarded by exposure to a steady flow of high-level exegetical content. All contain articles in English; most are written exclusively in English. The journals in alphabetical order are:

> *Biblica*
> *Catholic Biblical Quarterly*
> *Expository Times*
> *Interpretation*
> *Journal for the Study of the Old Testament*
> *Journal of Biblical Literature*
> *Revue Biblique*
> *Vetus Testamentum*
> *Westminster Theological Journal*
> *Zeitschrift für die alttestamentliche Wissenschaft*

**11.c.** *Old Testament Introductions*

The various one-volume introductions to the OT provide the fastest means of access to a discussion of significant critical (exegetically oriented) points related to an OT book. In addition to Eissfeldt's incomparable *The Old Testament: An Introduction* (III.1.b), several other books are excellent and likely to be of substantial value if consulted in this manner. The following list represents most of the standard scholarly works available in English:

Bernhard W. Anderson, *Understanding the Old Testament;* 3d ed. (Prentice-Hall, 1975).

Gleason Archer, Jr., *A Survey of Old Testament Introduction* (Moody Press, 1964).

Georg Fohrer, *Introduction to the Old Testament* (Abingdon Press, 1968).

Norman K. Gottwald, *A Light to the Nations: An Introduction to the Old Testament* (Harper & Brothers, 1959).

Roland Kenneth Harrison, *Introduction to the Old Testament* (Wm. B. Eerdmans Publishing Co., 1969).

Otto Kaiser, *Introduction to the Old Testament* (Augsburg Publishing House, 1975).

J. Alberto Soggin, *Introduction to the Old Testament;* The Old Testament Library (Westminster Press, 1976).

Edward J. Young, *An Introduction to the Old Testament;* rev. ed. (Wm. B. Eerdmans Publishing Co., 1958).

A new introduction, ranking second only to Eissfeldt's in scope, is:

Brevard S. Childs, *Introduction to the Old Testament as Scripture* (Fortress Press, 1979).

**11.d.** *Commentaries*

Of the dozens of commentary series, certain sets stand out as especially exegetical in format and interest. Commentary series are not consistent; you must actually evaluate each volume on its own merits. A recent work that does provide a book-by-book listing of commentaries is:

Brevard S. Childs, *Old Testament Books for Pastor and Teacher* (Westminster Press, 1977).

See also the brief (37 pp.) listing in:

John Goldingay, *Old Testament Commentary Survey* (London: Theological Students Fellowship, 1975).

Three major commentary series are still of tremendous value, though now substantially dated.

Carl Friedrich Keil and Franz Delitzsch, *A Commentary on the Old Testament;* 10 vols. (repr. Wm. B. Eerdmans Publishing Co., 1975).

*International Critical Commentary on the Holy Scriptures* (Charles Scribner's Sons, 1896–1951).

*The Interpreter's Bible;* 12 vols. (Abingdon Press, 1951–1957).

Of the several fine one-volume Bible commentaries, two may be mentioned as especially useful:

Donald Guthrie et al. (eds.), *The New Bible Commentary: Revised* (3d rev. ed.); (William B. Eerdmans Publishing Co., 1970);

Raymond E. Brown et al. (eds.), *The Jerome Biblical Commentary* (Prentice-Hall, 1968).

The best, most recent exegetically oriented commentary series are all as yet incomplete. Notable are:

*The Anchor Bible* (Doubleday & Co., 1964– ).

*Hermeneia* (Fortress Press, 1971– ).

*The New International Commentary on the Old Testament* (Wm. B. Eerdmans Publishing Co., 1955–).

*The Old Testament Library* (Westminster Press, 1961– ).

### 11.e. *Bible Dictionaries*

Several excellent Bible dictionaries furnish information on books, topics, themes, and words of Scripture. Of these, three deserve special mention as particularly suited to the interests of the exegete. The best, most comprehensive, and "standard" is:

George A. Buttrick (ed.), *The Interpreter's Dictionary of the Bible;* 4 vols. (Abingdon Press, 1962).

To this outstanding set a one-volume supplement has been added:

Keith Crim (ed.), *The Interpreter's Dictionary of the Bible,* Supplementary Volume (Abingdon Press, 1976).

Also excellent, and independently valuable for its contrasting point of view (conservative) on many exegetical issues, is:

Merrill C. Tenney (gen. ed.), *The Zondervan Pictorial Encyclopedia of the Bible;* 5 vols. (Zondervan Publishing House, 1975).

The finest one-volume Bible dictionary for the exegete is:

J. D. Douglas (organizing ed.), *The New Bible Dictionary* (Wm. B. Eerdmans Publishing Co., 1962; with updated bibliographies, 1965).

Although often brief in scope, the NBD is of the highest scholarly reliability.

### 11.f. *Other Aids*

A most welcome series of academic aids is in progress of publication by Fortress Press. These include many of the titles mentioned elsewhere in this primer. They explain in a readable, concise format such techniques as textual criticism, form criticism, literary criticism (including source criticism), and structural analysis. The series is:

Gene Tucker (ed.), Guides to Biblical Scholarship: Old Testament Series (Fortress Press, 1971– ).

Two major collections of illustrations relating to OT studies, each with thorough indexes, are often of value to the exegete. If you are analyzing a passage that mentions a site, a coin, a weight, an animal, a piece of furniture, a utensil, a weapon, or any place or object that might just "come alive" if illustrated, check these volumes to see if such an illustration might exist.

James B. Pritchard, *The Ancient Near East in Pictures Relating to the Old Testament* (Princeton University Press, 1954).

Some of the same illustrations are contained in a selection and combination of pictures from the above and texts from Pritchard's *Ancient Near Eastern Texts Relating to the Old Testament* (see III.4.a):

James B. Pritchard, *The Ancient Near East: An Anthology of Texts and Pictures* (Princeton University Press, 1958).

The second major collection is:

Clifford M. Jones, *Old Testament Illustrations* (Cambridge University Press, 1971).

On the area of the Dead Sea Scrolls, a most useful publication has appeared:

Joseph A. Fitzmyer, *The Dead Sea Scrolls: Major Publications and Tools for Study* (Society of Biblical Literature and Scholars Press, 1975).

Fitzmyer introduces the various texts, explains where they and their translations are published, and outlines the contents of some of the major scrolls. He also provides an excellent bibliography and an index to biblical passages in the scrolls.

The best translation of the major Dead Sea Scrolls is found in:

Theodor H. Gaster, *The Dead Sea Scriptures: In English Translation with Introduction and Notes;* 3d ed. rev. & enl. (Doubleday & Co., Anchor Books, 1976).

Finally, when you need guidance to bibliographic resources more broadly within the general field of theological study (church history, systematic theology, practical theology, missions, etc.—including biblical studies), the most comprehensive guide available is:

John A. Bollier, *The Literature of Theology: A Guide for Students and Pastors* (Westminster Press, 1979).

## 12. APPLICATION

### 12.a. *Hermeneutics*

Hermeneutics is the theory of understanding a passage's meaning. At virtually every stage of an exegesis, you are using hermeneutical (interpretational) principles, whether implicitly or explicitly. At the application stage, however, it is most important of all to be absolutely clear about the interpretational principles you employ since a proper application depends so greatly on reasonable and honest use of good principles. In other words, the rules you go by to interpret the passage will largely determine how accurately you apply the passage.

Traditionally—and simplistically—four different kinds of meanings have been discovered in biblical passages: (1) The literal (historical) meaning; (2) The allegorical (mystical or "spiritual") meaning; (3) The anagogic (typological—especially as relating to the end times and eternity) meaning; and (4) The tropological (moral) meaning. Precisely because the literal meaning was understood so narrowly (as merely the meaning the passage once had rather than what it may also mean now), interpreters were driven to seek something personal, contemporary, and practical from the latter three types of meaning. After all, we read the Bible for help in our *own* lives, not just as a historical exercise. The latter types of meaning (allegorical, anagogic, tropological), however, are not usually directly derived from the passage itself, but tend to be more or less invented by the imagination according to rules not always consistently applied. Such kinds of interpretations are often seductively appealing, and can allow otherwise "dull" passages to seem to speak personally and practically. Unfortunately, however, they usually ignore the intentionality of the text itself, so that what the ancient inspired author intended to be understood from his or her writing is grossly exceeded, indeed, eclipsed by almost uncontrolled mystical, typological and moralizing sorts of over-interpretation.

The delicate task of the interpreter, then, is to be sure that everything the passage means is brought out, but that nothing additional is read into the passage. We don't want to miss anything, but we don't want to "find" anything that isn't really there, either. Hermeneutics properly applied, is thus interested in the boundaries of interpretation—the upper and lower limits—which are intended by the Spirit of God for the reader.

Hundreds of volumes have been written on hermeneutics, most of them offering at least some helpful methodology. Perhaps the most balanced work, maintaining a high regard for the authority and inspiration of the entire Bible is:

A. Berkeley Mickelsen, *Interpreting the Bible* (Wm.
   B. Eerdmans Publishing Co., 1963).

In addition, a number of recent works on the hermeneutical task as it applies to preaching may be cited as particularly useful in their respective categories.

An encouragement toward the responsible extraction from a text of those features that will bring to a congregation a real sense of involvement in the "original" audience of scriptural events is:

> Wayne E. Ward, *The Word Comes Alive* (Broadman Press, 1969).

For a brief essay with helpful examples of so-called "expository" preaching see:

> Alan A. Stibbs, *Expounding God's Word* (Wm. B. Eerdmans Publishing Co., 1961).

An insightful book on many aspects of OT preaching is:

> Elizabeth Achtemeier, *The Old Testament and the Proclamation of the Gospel* (Westminster Press, 1973).

Perhaps the best single introduction to the methodology of expository preaching, with step-by-step guidance for actual sermon preparation, is:

> James W. Cox, *A Guide to Biblical Preaching* (Abingdon Press, 1976).

### 12.b. *Some Do's and Don'ts in Application*

1. *Do* consider the needs and composition of your audience in the way that you construct the application.
2. *Do* be careful that the application derives directly and logically from the passage (in other words, respect the passage's intentionality).
3. *Do* try to limit yourself if possible to the central or priority application.
4. *Do*—if your passage functions primarily to illustrate a principle stated elsewhere in Scripture—be sure to demonstrate a genuine relationship between the two.

1. *Don't* multiply applications needlessly (more is not necessarily better).

2. *Don't* assume that your audience will automatically make a proper application of the passage just because the rest of your exegesis is good.

3. *Don't* invent an application if none seems forthcoming. Better to say nothing rather than something misleading.

4. *Don't* confuse illumination with inspiration. The former refers to what you alone, emotionally, existentially, and individually may derive from the passage; the latter refers to what God has intended that the passage say to any of us in general. For illumination you should diligently appropriate for yourself a most precious, life-sustaining resource of the student and pastor, for which exegesis could never hope to substitute—prayer.